THE CULT OF THE VICTIM-VETERAN

The Cult of the Victim-Veteran explores the pool of American post-Vietnam War angst that rightists began plying in the 1980s. Ronald Reagan's 1984 proclamation of a new "Morning in America" encoded the war as the moment of the nation's fall from grace; it was the meme plagiarized by Donald Trump for his "Make America Great Again" (MAGA) slogan.

The national funk tapped for right-wing revanchism was psychologized when George H.W. Bush appropriated post-Vietnam syndrome, the diagnostic forerunner to post-traumatic stress disorder (PTSD), to memorialize the military accomplishments in the Persian Gulf War of 1990–1991—we had "kicked the Vietnam Syndrome." America was a victim-nation, its trauma emblemized by PTSD-stricken veterans whose war mission had been lost on the home front, cast aside, even spat on, upon return home.

In this book we see the long historical threads woven for MAGA: the twining of traditional and modern ways of knowing that imbues war trauma with political and cultural properties that complicate its diagnostic use; the post-World War I disclosure that many shellshock patients had never been exposed to exploding shells, and the use of wounded-veteran imagery to fan the flames of German fascism; the cultural necessity of reimaging antiwar Vietnam veterans as psychiatric casualties that calls forth a new diagnostic category, PTSD; the derivatizing of PTSD for traumatic brain injury, Agent Orange, and moral injury; and the victim-veteran figure as metaphor for a wounded America, for which MAGA is the remedy.

Jerry Lembcke is the author of eight books including *The Spitting Image: Myth, Memory, and the Legacy of Vietnam* (NYU Press, 1998) and *Hanoi Jane: War, Sex, and Fantasies of Betrayal* (UMass Press, 2010). He is presently Associate Professor of Sociology Emeritus at Holy Cross College in Worcester, Massachusetts, and Distinguished Lecturer for the Organization of American Historians.

THE CULT OF THE VICTIM-VETERAN

MAGA Fantasies in Lost-war America

Jerry Lembcke

Routledge
Taylor & Francis Group

NEW YORK AND LONDON

First published 2024
by Routledge
605 Third Avenue, New York, NY 10158

and by Routledge
4 Park Square, Milton Park, Abingdon, Oxon, OX14 4RN

Routledge is an imprint of the Taylor & Francis Group, an informa business

© 2024 Jerry Lembcke

Library of Congress Cataloging-in-Publication Data
Names: Lembcke, Jerry, 1943– author.
Title: The cult of the victim-veteran : MAGA fantasies in lost-war America / Jerry Lembcke.
Other titles: MAGA fantasies in lost-war America
Description: New York, NY : Routledge, 2023. |
Includes bibliographical references and index. |
Identifiers: LCCN 2023004126 (print) | LCCN 2023004127 (ebook) |
ISBN 9781032490267 (hardback) | ISBN 9781032490243 (paperback) |
ISBN 9781003391906 (ebook)
Subjects: LCSH: Veterans–Psychology. | Post-traumatic stress disorder. |
Veterans–Mental health–United States. | Veterans–Political activity–United States. |
Disabled veterans–Mental health–United States.
Classification: LCC U22.3 .L44 2023 (print) | LCC U22.3 (ebook) |
DDC 355.0019–dc23/eng/20230329
LC record available at https://lccn.loc.gov/2023004126
LC ebook record available at https://lccn.loc.gov/2023004127

ISBN: 9781032490267 (hbk)
ISBN: 9781032490243 (pbk)
ISBN: 9781003391906 (ebk)

DOI: 10.4324/9781003391906

Typeset in Bembo
by Newgen Publishing UK

To Writers Who Write What Needs to be Read

CONTENTS

ACKNOWLEDGMENTS

My greatest debts are owed to the scholars, journalists, and filmmakers referenced in endnotes. Thanks to Michael Gibson and Dean Birkenkamp at Routledge for giving the book a shot. I am grateful for the patience (with me) of librarians Eileen Cravedi and Philippe Telemaque at Holy Cross College. Administrative Assistant Paula Hall's cheery can-do presence was always appreciated. Ellis Jones and Daina Harvey managed my beer list—thanks. Many thanks to the painter, potter, poet, Carolyn Howe, for encouragement and editing.

INTRODUCTION

If there had never been a Shellshock Cinema after World War I, would shellshock have endured as an emblem of war trauma? If the *New York Times* had not attributed Vietnam veteran protests at the 1972 Republican Party convention to their "post-war shock," would there be a post-traumatic stress disorder (PTSD) in the *Diagnostic and Statistical Manual* (DSM)? Had the Central Park Jogger crime story not gotten reframed as a trauma story, would we have ever heard of veterans with traumatic brain injury (TBI)? And had the imagery of traumatized and discarded war veterans not pervaded representations of America's lost wars, would the revanchist sentiments of MAGA ever found footing?

Easily dismissed as rhetorical turns, these questions nevertheless point to an association between arousing goings-on outside of scientific discourse—spectacles—and the seminal thinking on new medical terminology. The core chapters of this book reveal that the decisive events in the development of war trauma language have always occurred far from examination rooms and research parks. Without the elements of spectacle provided by stage performers, photographers, filmmakers, and news organizations, it is unlikely that the protocols of science themselves would have brought shellshock, PTSD, TBI, moral injury, or even Agent Orange (AO) poisoning into our conversation.

The book presents its subject matter more or less chronologically in the order in which the various diagnoses appeared to public and professional audiences from the Enlightenment to the present. Before getting to the role of spectacle in the making of war-trauma diagnoses, three other dimensions of that relationship are considered. First is the interplay of spectacle in the emergence of science itself. Spectacles are almost synonymous with the emotive side of human existence, appreciated mostly as reminders of a primal stage through which we passed on our way to modernity in which the mindful rationality of science is characteristic; but

DOI: 10.4324/9781003391906-1

a look at the actual history of their relationship reveals their greater compatibility. Indeed, right into the twenty-first century we can see instances of spectacle and science abiding one another quite amiably.

Second is the consideration given war by Anastasia Baklogianni and Valerie M. Hope in their edited volume *War as Spectacle: Ancient and Modern Perspectives on the Display of Armed Conflict*. Viewed as the authors do, war becomes the spectacle-of-all-spectacles that makes it the primogenitor of, not only all else in the twining of spectacle and war trauma, but the origins in ancient cultures of the very notion of spectacle as we think of it today.

The third revisits the post-World War II literature on the appeal that Nazi spectacles had to the European masses in the lead-up to fascism in the middle of the twentieth century. Informed by the work of Marxist and Freudian classicists, that literature was made resonant for the post-World War II period by the Frankfurt School theorists, Max Horkheimer and Theodore Adorno. In their work we see spectacle positioned not just as complicit in the construction of mental health nomenclature but, as well, as a technology of propaganda that preyed upon the interwar anxieties and paranoias—themselves symptoms of trauma left by The Great War. The sequence of war-begets-trauma which is then exploited for propaganda purposes to foment more war appears to be repeating itself in twenty-first-century America. This is one of the concerns animating this book.

The book forms, thereby, a several-legged approach to its subject that sets in relief the seminal role of spectacle in the biographies of war-trauma diagnoses, a role that often overshadows that of science. It is an approach that also considers the less-than-pure distinction between science and spectacle—certainly *less* pure than the mental health establishment would have us believe. It is an approach in which we see how war-trauma representations get twisted into pro-war propaganda that turns wounded veterans themselves into spectacles that are used to incite more war. With the thread of war-as-spectacle running through it, it is an approach, admittedly, that threatens, at times, to conflate explanandums and explanans— but such is the messiness of real-world social studies.

Chapter 3 is the first of the core chapters on the role of spectacle in the social construction of PTSD, AO, TBI, and moral injury as notions at play in the diagnosis of war trauma. PTSD traced a meteoric trajectory out of the 1960s when diagnostic manuals had no page for war trauma. From stock First World War shellshock imagery and their own imaginations, screenwriters began molding twitchy and emotionally damaged Vietnam veterans hallucinating jungle warfare in films such as *Motor Psycho* (1965). Journalists and mental health workers fashioned these prototypes into post-Vietnam syndrome, the 1970s forerunner to PTSD.

By the 1970s, thousands of Vietnam veterans were marching in the streets with war protesters and adopting the dress and mannerisms of the counterculture. The antiwar warriors were a spectacle. They challenged traditional standards of masculine behavior and presented a counterpoint to Washington's claim that opposition to the war was disrespectful to the troops themselves. In the political context of the times, stigmatizing dissident veterans as psychiatric casualties was more practical than prosecuting them. The psychiatric profession answered the call to service and armored-up with new diagnostic nomenclature. Its quintessentially socially constructed product, PTSD, was ready for the 1980 DSM of the American Psychiatric Association.

AO burst into public awareness in the late 1970s. Having morphed from an innocuous and obscure label for an herbicide used by the US military in Vietnam into a symbol for environmental activism, it then leaped definitional boundaries for an association with war trauma: a noun for a chemical agent had shape-shifted to a pseudo-diagnostic category—as if a veteran could now *have* the affliction, AO.

In the political climate of the post-war years, the fusion of AO's chemical and cultural properties functioned as an antidote to the movement of antiwar veterans. Spectacular photographs of deforestation and human birth defects ginned emotions that flowed into the trauma discourse of PTSD. That mixing was stirred by Chicago CBS affiliate WBBM's 1978 news special *Agent Orange: Vietnam's Deadly Fog*, and its remake for the 1986 film *Unnatural Causes: The Agent Orange Story*, starring John Ritter; it was the film that transformed the documentarian character of the story into entertainment spectacle. In Chapter 4 we see the interplay of political, scientific, and informational forces that pushed AO onto the stage of war-trauma discourse.

TBI moved from a lowercase and meaningless word combination with an incidental presence in a few news stories in the 1980s into the media spotlight with the Central Park Jogger story. The "Jogger," as she was known for weeks, was a young attractive investment banker allegedly beaten and raped by black men while running in New York City's Central Park in 1989. With news that she suffered head injuries from the attack, reportage shifted from themes of race and crime to medical narratives that debuted TBI for professional and public audiences.

Even through the Jogger phase of TBI's biography, it had no association with war injuries; and with public fascination with her eventually fading, the disconnect might have endured. But the spectacle of glamor-boy NFL quarterbacks with head injuries was not likely to fade so quickly. Breaking with news of injuries to Troy Aikman and Steve Young in the late 1990s, gave TBI a second wind that carried into the war news.

When ABC newscaster Bob Woodward was wounded in Iraq by an improvised explosive device, TBI was garlanded the "signature wound of the war in Iraq." A handsome newscaster disfigured by the war's signature wound was a spectacle that news organizations could not resist. Virtually every television outlet broadcast a "TBI Special" and every newspaper featured lengthy and detailed reports on the technologies, medical insights, and human dramas spawned by the novel condition TBI—an outpouring of attention that one media critic labeled "war porn."

Like with PTSD, news media and popular culture paved the road for TBI's entry to medical practice. But leading professionals were skeptical of its validity. Dr. Charles Hoge, for example, wrote in a 2009 *New England Journal of Medicine* article, that post-concussive symptoms of Iraq War veterans were more strongly correlated with PTSD and depression than with concussion. Hoge's report was reminiscent of World War I veterans with the symptoms of shellshock who had never been exposed to exploding shells. Nevertheless, and as was the case with shellshock, TBI's cache as a cultural category gave it legs that took it into America's post-war story, far beyond its place in war-trauma literature.

Moral injury enters the war trauma conversation from literary studies even further outside science than the other categories considered here. The science of war trauma has long been driven by—and bedeviled by—the search for "biomarkers" that would validate war trauma as a *real* malady. So-called brain lesions associated with shellshock proved chimeric; the absence of an observable, anatomical disorder undermined the validity of PTSD; hope that fMRIs and EEG tracings could reveal neurological disruptions due to war violence has never been realized. As they stand today, war-trauma studies are as much a cultural form as a scientific practice.

The abandonment of scientific discourse in favor of non-cartesian ways of knowing the political landscape is not new. In 1990, President George Bush justified sending US troops to the Persian Gulf with a list of reasons that included the defense of Saudi Arabia, the liberation of Kuwait, the removal of Saddam Hussain, and jobs. When none of these proved persuasive to voters—and after he had sent the troops—he collapsed means-end logic and made the means of war, the troops themselves, the reason for the war.

Moral injury is a rhetorical ploy with comparable scientific weightlessness and strategic purpose: with only tenuous validation of war trauma diagnoses in hand, it takes an about face and marches in the other direction toward philosophical musings on war, shame, guilt, and human nature.

Donald Trump's Make America Great Again (MAGA) movement was conceived and birthed in America's lost-war culture. Lingering feelings that the country had defeated itself in Vietnam and turned against the men who fought there resonated with a public frustrated with losses accruing in the Middle East and suspicions the government knew more about the illnesses soldiers returned with than it was admitting.

Chapter 7 ties together the betrayal themes born in the years after Vietnam with those arising in the twenty-first-century wars. The connecting threads are the specters of veterans with unseen wounds for which "trauma" is the signifier and, in turn, the cause of the societal malaise for which MAGA is the presumptive prescription.

1

SPECTACLE, SCIENCE, AND WAR TRAUMA

MAGA's Tangled Back Stories

> We, as historians, need to resist the temptation of discriminating between "real science" or its legitimate precursors and public spectacle.
> (Bernadette Bensaude-Vincent and Christine Blondel, *Science and Spectacle in the European Enlightenment*)[1]

> War conceptualized as spectacle leads us to question the very nature of viewership, and its moral and esthetical dimensions.
> (Anastasia Bakogianni, *War as Spectacle*)[2]

But are spectacle and science really so separable? Historians who have looked at their relationship over many centuries see something more complicated, even an interplay between the two. There are times, in fact, when one was put in the service of the other. In the late nineteenth century, for example, theatrical performances, spectacles, were staged by a French psychiatrist to publicize hysteria as a diagnostic concept. In the 1950s, the *Wow!* factor in science would be harnessed for spectacles that the new medium of television exploited for commercial value.[3]

The critical reflections on science coming out of cultural studies in recent years have made clear that the history of science was tangled from the beginning with philosophical studies of nature, the mind, and the origins of what became the mental health professions. A review of that history leads to the late nineteenth century when spectacle-making of mental health patients foretold the post-World War I construction of shellshock imagery that found its way into lost-war propaganda that fueled German fascism. In the years leading to the Second World War, that imagery grounded betrayal narratives for national defeat that lured millions of Europeans down a path of vindictiveness with apocalyptic consequences.

DOI: 10.4324/9781003391906-2

And the beat goes on. The war in Vietnam begat a new diagnostic concept, post-traumatic stress disorder (PTSD). By 2020, PTSD's prominence as the fourth most common psychiatric diagnosis in America overshadowed its origins in the 1970s as a concept designed for Vietnam veterans. Veterans who joined in protests of the war were viewed as psychological casualties, victims of war trauma.

Going forward, the victim-veteran imagery would rouse the public belief that political and cultural trends at home had undermined the military mission in Vietnam; and just as the notion of shellshock had energized European movements to avenge the losses of World War I, the spectacle of trauma-stricken veterans would enrich a twenty-first-century movement to make America great again.

Spectacle: Bridging Tradition and Enlightenment

The Enlightenment was a European intellectual movement of the seventeenth and eighteenth centuries that galvanized the lines that had been forming for centuries between Eastern and Western modes of thought. As described by historian Irving Zeitlin, Western civilization had distinguished itself in opposition to the "fetishism, animistic, and magical beliefs" characteristic of the "enchanted gardens" of the East. The sixteenth-century advent of Protestant religion in the West consolidated what Max Horkheimer and Theodor Adorno called in the *Dialectic of Enlightenment* the "disenchantment of the world" with a form of rationalism that dissolved myths and substituted knowledge for fancy.[4]

Knowledge not fancy—the clarion call for intellectual war against intolerance and dogma, and the call for science as the antidote to medieval superstition. And yet, in an effort to demonstrate the superiority of science as a way to know the world, its devotees staged public demonstrations, spectacles, tapping into peoples' fears and wonderments of the natural world that were rooted in traditional practices and religious beliefs. "The power of visual experience," write Bernadette Bensaude-Vincent and Christine Blondel in *Science and Spectacle in the European Enlightenment*, was "legitimized by the prevailing empiricist philosophy claiming that all ideas originated in sensations."

> If knowledge entered the mind through the senses, then public demonstrations were the best form of pedagogy … Vision was the most important sense in the Enlightenment period [but] sensibility also formed part of the epistemic strategies of the Enlightenment. Admiration and repulsion, the sense of the sublime and the sense of horror, all such aesthetic emotions aroused by tragedy were occasionally mobilized by public demonstration.[5]

Indeed, Bensaude-Vincent and Blondel go on to write, that Louis Bernard Le Bovier de Fontenelle described by them as "the founding father of science communication," thought nature was made a spectacle to be performed on stage as a way to advance the power of science in order to display "God's magnificence"—a cleverly worded strategy of his to exploit *pre*modern dispositions for the "selling" of science as the essence of modernism.[6] The irony of that strategy, as captured by Linda Scott, was in using the power of image to muster emotions that would bypass rational thought in order to convince viewers that rational thought was superior to emotions as a way to know the world—emotions deployed to discredit the power of emotions![7]

We also see that irony in the way public audiences were enchanted in the interest of *dis*enchanting their traditional cultures of knowing. With the role of science in promoting modernism being to *dis*enchant the world, as Horkheimer and Adorno put it, it is then with great interest that we read an epigraph for a museum collection of apparatuses devised to display the power of science which says they were used to *enchant* the audiences that had assembled for demonstrations of science's awesomeness. The assemblies, known as salons at the time, were held in workshops or theaters, and drew the social and intellectual elites of the day:

> salons were often [a] theater of glittering "electrical evenings" in which ladies and gentlemen amused themselves by experimenting—even on their own bodies—with attraction, repulsion, shocks, and sparks. In the darkened rooms, traveling "electrifiers" put on theatrical performances that used ingenious devices to display darting snakes of fire, luminescent letters, and aurora borealis in glass jars. Experiments followed one another in a dizzying sequence that also included sparks from Franklin's bells, a blast from Volta's pistol, and the spectacular explosion of the "thunder house." [8]

It was the Salons' performance of unified opposites represented by public fascinations with nature—snakes, lightening, and the urges of their own bodies—and equally fascinating technological wonders of modern technology—bell jars containing lightening!—that composed the dialectic of the Enlightenment that Horkheimer and Adorno captured with the title of their book. It was a synthesis that would unravel with World War II and confound medical science into the twenty-first century.

The synthesis of traditional and modern cultural motifs, cognitive and emotive ways of knowing, was nowhere more interesting than in the fields of health science and medicine. In his article "Honore Fragonard, Anatomical Virtuoso," historian Jonathon Simon remarks on sixteenth-century controversies surrounding "public dissection as performance and spectacle," which accompanied studies of human anatomy. "Looking at Enlightenment anatomy from the perspective of the *spectacle* of human anatomy," he writes, we see not "the ineluctable progress of medical science," while getting a clearer view of modern medicine" (emphasis in the original).[9]

The spectacle of anatomical displays continued into the eighteenth century when they were "very present in the public culture of Paris," according to Simon. Their popularity was driven by their entertainment value and peoples' fascinations with Nature that dovetailed with the interests of the Parisian elite in the *philosophes*. Members of "the polite society" were encouraged to "dissect real human corpses themselves," and the sculptor Honore Fragonard used dead bodies as models for his wax figures, the most famous of which is his "Horse and Rider."[10]

Simon notes the tension between the modernist utility of anatomical studies demonstrated by public viewings of cadavers and the wax models made from them, on the one hand, and the affective appeal they had to audiences, on the other. The popularity of their stagings, he says, derived only in part from scientific interest, while their aesthetic quality was applauded as "a triumph of artisanal virtuosity." The models evoked pre-Reformation sentiments reminiscent of Catholic Church reaction to the protestant movement, and their acceptance by the public as a kind of art form was regarded by some critics within the scientific community at the time as a distraction—a decidedly *not* modern muse.[11]

More a mutually defining interplay between modern science and traditional impulses than tension, as described by Simon, the science—not-science divide in ways of knowing would occupy epistemologists throughout the nineteenth and twentieth centuries. But the defeat of the United States by Vietnamese peasant forces and the stagnation of advanced capitalist societies at the turn to the twenty-first century raised questions about the enlightenment notion of "progress"—how far had modern societies really come? At the same time, how superior was science as an approach to understanding the world?

Robert Kaplan's 2022 book *Adriatic* reiterated the postmodernist assertion that the modern era had reached a dead end; David Graeber and David Wengrow's *The Dawn of Everything* in 2021 even questioned whether the enlightenment itself was as distinct from indigenous and traditional societies, as is commonly believed; and Benjamin Teitelbaum's 2020 *War for Eternity* pointed to the twenty-first-century neo-fascist movement that draws followers with philosophical tenets known as Traditionalism as evidence for the vitality of the *pre*-modern in modern life. The spectacles of President Donald Trump shrugging-off modern medicine during the Covid-19 crisis, his dismissal of climate change as a hoax, and his valuing of personal loyalty over expertise are indicative of Traditionalism's appeal to him; that his expressions attract millions of followers is indicative of modernism's loose grip on the American collective conscience.[12]

The whistles and bells of commercial culture may have obscured the longing of some Americans for ways of thinking about their lives outside the box of scientific rationality and credentialed expertise—religious notions of revelation, after all, have a longer lifespan than modern science. While Donald Trump surely spoke to voter frustrations with job cuts, immigration policy, and the digitalizing of their world, he also touched latent feelings that the past—the 1950s, if not the 1500s of the Traditionalists—might offer a way forward. These were the feelings that Trump harnessed for his MAGA movement.

The mass's rally to MAGA's retro appeal seemed to surprise journalists and political elites. And yet, in a field with which most Americans are intimately familiar—health care—the histories reveal that the braiding of spectacle and reason has remained a constant for centuries. The history of war trauma diagnoses, with their sex and gender themes and political implications, is especially telling, in that regard. Shellshock patients in the First World War are the centerpiece in that story, but the notion of shellshock is underwritten by studies of male hysteria at Hospital Salpêtrière in Paris in the late nineteenth century.

A *Visuel* Leads the Way in the "Science" of Mental Health

Prior to the beginning of industrialization in the early 1800s, the field of mental health practice as we know it today was little known. The social isolation of rural life that came with peasant and family-farm production and scattered-site small-scale manufacturing likely resulted in injuries to single workers that went unreported or even unrecognized. The cultures of self-sufficiency that those conditions bred, moreover, meant that treatments for the emotional effects of accidents—"nerves" was the expression common to the times—were the responsibility of the injured parties, a practice that sometimes made victims easy targets for hucksters selling "nerve tonics."[13] In fact, some of those symptoms were consistent with hysteria, the female disorder to which men were thought to be immune.

It was the developments in transportation and communication associated with the industrial revolution, and not science itself, that began breaking down the taboo on male hysteria. Railway accidents were among the first appearances of modernism's downside: large numbers of people aggregated by the new technology, in ways they had never been before, and put at risk in relatively fast-moving wood-frame train cars. People's injuries following accidents were then widely publicized by the new medium of mass-produced newspapers. And with that was born a new expression of spectacle.

Soon thereafter, a previously unknown disorder called "railway spine" appeared, its claimants not always evincing physical injury, or even evidence of having actually been in a train accident. The common symptoms of railway spine included spinal rigidity that prevented bending forward; an exaggerated concavity of the lower back, with the pelvis thrust forward and the shoulders thrown back as if the body was bracing for impact from behind; unsteadiness when standing or walking; a "peculiar gait" with one foot appearing to flop uncontrollably to the ground, and a leg that seemed to drag the ground in less than full strikes. The appearances of symptoms in men when no physical injuries were evident pointed to a psychological dimension in railway spine, the study of which eventually breached the reluctance of doctors to put "male" and "hysteria" in the same sentences.[14]

Working at the Hospital Salpêtrière in the late 1800s, the French psychiatrist Jean-Martin Charcot considered the cases of men impaired from industrial accidents and theorized that fright alone could be the cause of their symptoms. In effect, Charcot was suggesting that men could be hysterical and that, in keeping with their nature of being more physically active than women, their symptoms were more likely to take the form of bodily contortions—like railway spine. He even called one type of male hysteria "clownisme," a name that cultural studies Professor Elaine Showalter says reflected his lifelong fascination with circus clowns.[15]

Charcot's reference to clownisme invited the imagery of entertainment and forms of street theater that predated modernism. It's presence as a prompt for Charcot suggests also that he saw an element of performance in patients' presentation of symptoms, a mixing of voluntary and involuntary causes, mental and physiological sources for what he observed. As an influence on his approach to patients, clownisme recollected the same kind of traditional cultural imagery that inspired the physical and biological sciences a hundred years earlier and would continue to work their affective ways in the new sciences of mental health.

And like the impresarios of science who preceded him, Charcot, too, drew on religious art of the premodern era that had sought to portray mental psychopathologies as matters of the mind–body relationship. It was thus, as Sander Gilman wrote, that troubles of the interior mind were thought to be observable as features on the external body—and therefore subject to representation through illustration and art. "By the Renaissance," according to him, "the *appearance* of the mentally ill … is seen as a classifiable, interpretable reference to [the individual's] mental state (emphasis added)."[16] The presumption that insanity, or any mental state, could be *seen* as per the title of Gilman's book *Seeing the Insane*, was consistent with the empiricism inherited by modernism that privileged the sense of sight in scientific method and the role of spectacle in its promotion.

And what was *seen* mingled the enchantments of Baroque art forms and Enlightenment science. At "the close of the seventeenth century," writes Gilman, the iconography of insanity, which is to say the way it was visualized, was well established and the images *in medical texts* were "identical with those in fine and popular arts (emphasis added)." To illustrate his point, Gilman displays a diagram from the Middle Ages showing the postures of the maniac, the epileptic, the melancholic, and the frenetic, postures similar to those treated for hysteria in the nineteenth century.[17]

Charcot was a neurologist who by training and cultural proclivities was a man-for-the-times. He came to the study of hysteria with a theory drawn from the classical model that linked mind and body. Early on, Charcot suspected that physical impairment of the brain, such as might be caused by an injury or a wound, was responsible for the bodily disorder exhibited by his patients. Known as the "brain lesion" theory, this idea came under attack after doctors practicing hypnosis were able to show that physical symptoms could be induced in otherwise healthy subjects by the utterance of suggestive words, and that ailing patients could be relieved of their symptoms by other suggestions. The odd and inexplicable behaviors associated with hysteria, in other words, had a more attenuated relationship to the physical condition of the brain than the lesions theory would predict—an insight that Sigmund Freud would build on a few years later.

Charcot also had a bent for spectacle. Described by Elaine Showalter as "a showman with great theatrical flair," he began weekly demonstrations at Salpêtrière in the 1870s involving public lectures and displays of hysterical patients. He used his artwork to decorate the "stage" and cast hysterical patients as the stars of the show. In front of audiences as large as five hundred he would imitate the behavior of patients he was about the present and then bring to the stage women suffering the conditions he had mimicked. In one instance, writes Showalter, when he planned to discuss tremors, "he brought in three women wearing hats and long feathers, each of which trembled in a way characteristic of the disease." On another occasion, Charcot led women he diagnosed as hysterics before audiences and had his interns hypnotize them. A Swedish doctor reported later:

one woman `would crawl on all fours on the floor barking furiously like a dog when told she was a dog ... Another would walk with a top hat in her arms rocking it to and fro and kissing it tenderly when she was told it was her baby.[18]

Reminiscent of the public demonstrations of electricity in an earlier period, Charcot left his audiences spellbound, "Everything in his lectures," recalled one of his students, "was designed to attract attention and captivate the audience by means of visual and auditory impressions."[19]

Critics would eventually allege that Charcot had "invented" hysteria through the power of his theatrics but, just as railway spine was a product of its times-of-origin, so too hysteria was propelled to prominence by the technological and cultural forces changing Europe in the late nineteenth century. Charcot, moreover, worked within the milieu of medical science already altered by modernism and the influence of railway spine studies. Charcot was also in harmony with secular movements against Catholicism and the church's practice of exorcism to treat diabolic possession and other precursors to hysteria. Additionally, the centralization of manufacture and transportation in the early decades of the century had changed the relationships between workers, employers, media, and the state. Factory production was pulling women off farms, putting them into cities where their presence in the workplace challenged the traditional boundaries of sex and gender—men at work, women at home—putting stresses on working-class women who were alone and sexually vulnerable in urban environments new to them.[20]

The Camera: Heaven-sent for Spectacle in the Science of Mental Health

The invention of photography led to its first use by Hugh Diamond in the women's department of the Surrey County Lunatic Asylum where he was superintendent in the 1850s. The photograph, Diamond argued, could record with greater accuracy than hand-drawn portraits the external manifestations, observed on the body, of internal derangements, although Gilman observes that the photographs chosen by doctors for inclusion in textbooks of the time sometimes resembled the same postures and positions established by the tradition of portraiture over the years.[21]

Charcot hired photographer Albert Londe to record the postures of hysterics and some of those were sold with sketches for public consumption. Above all else, it was the primacy of "the visual," the photographic image as spectacle, that it brought to symptomology that reinforced the idea that psychological states could register visually on the body—and specifically as facial expressions—bolstering the foundation on which the sub-genre of psychosomatic illnesses would be identified, studied, and treated. The aestheticism that attached to the photographs, moreover, lent hysteria the necessary cachet for appeal to popular cultural interests outside the narrow community of professional diagnosticians.[22]

It's not so certain, of course, that photography had to precede hysteria in the same sense that theater had to precede demonstrations of science, or that there could have been no railway spine before there were railroads, but there is little doubt that the photographs of Charcot's patients enhanced the allure that his practice had for the public and other professionals. At that level, though, Charcot was merely demonstrating, 70 years ahead of Marshall McLuhan, that the "medium is the message," whereas the real significance of Salpêtrière was that the *medium was the method*: it was the presence of the camera that evoked from the patients the bodily expressions that were then said to be symptoms of hysteria.[23]

Historians who study the influence of Charcot's work on the practice of psychiatry going forward emphasize the interactions of the doctor, his artwork, his female patients, and the presence of the camera. The course of that influence ran through the worlds of art, theater, and novels from where they looped back into the cultures of medical practice and public policy. One of Charcot's patients was Blanche Wittman whose fits and convulsions were "painted, displayed, and photographed" and reported in detail for the Western medical community. Another was Augustine who began having seizures after being raped by her mother's lover; in the hospital Salpêtrière she became the most photographed of all of Londe's subjects and the inspiration for playwrights and screenwriters.

In turn, the images of Wittman and Augustine "taught other women how hysterics looked," according to Showalter. She quotes historian Jan Goldstein saying, "The 'iconography' of hysteria as defined by Charcot—with all its vividly theatrical contortions and grimaces—seems to have been so widely publicized … in both pictorial and verbal form, as to constitute for that historical moment a reigning 'cultural perception' of how to act when insane.'"[24] The classical paintings of demonic figures that surrounded Charcot and the women may have suggested to them the poses that he wanted to see, according to Michael Roth. But the more serious criticism of Charcot was that he actually "coached" his patients, and that by proffering them a "warped celebrity" when they executed his script—while yet keeping them confined in the hospital—he was coercing from them the presentation of symptoms that he then used to define hysteria. In time, novelists who may once have found their subject matter in Augustine found it in the practice of the doctor himself, the impresario who made it all happen.[25]

Charcot's use of photography had the unintended consequence of exposing the interplays of voluntary and involuntary factors in the production and presentation of patients' symptoms. With the mind in play, so to speak, it was a short step to consider the power of patients' imaginations in creating the symptoms seen by doctors, and the influence of cultural forces on those imaginations.[26]

Charcot's protégés, Freud among them, would take more literally the possibility that hysteria was a form of body language, expressions of feelings that social norms had banished from the mind and tongue to a level of the psyche called the "unconscious." From there, emotions stemming from the "unspeakable" and "unthinkable" reemerge as unwanted physical symptoms. The linkages made between mind, body, and society in that emerging paradigm provided a model for understanding how the news media, popular culture, and medical science fit together in the studies of war trauma, a paradigm that holds the key to understanding those same war-born maladies a century later.[27] Freud became skeptical of Charcot's ability to schematize the external manifestations of internal illnesses. He grew wary of the way that Charcot used illustrations to prove his claims and seldom used them himself. "Reacting to Charcot," wrote Gilman, "Freud banished the depiction of the insane [from his writings] as well as the study of the external phenomena of madness from psychoanalysis."[28]

But Freud was ahead of his time, for the *visuels* were not yet finished with their promotion of science as a spectacle. Londe's still photographs had been able to capture the facial contortions of Charcot's female patients, and thereby magnetize the attention of doctors on "the visual." In a sense, that part of what went on at Salpêtrière lent support for the idea that doctors believed, not just what they could see, but the visuals, the sights, they could document through illustration and photography.

The early twentieth century continued the comingling of art, science, and new technology. In her book *God or Gorilla: Images of Evolution in the Jazz Age*, Constance Clark documented the way scientific thinking was popularized through cartoons and illustrations, noting as well that "visual images colored the way scientists themselves thought about evolution." And just as then-new technologies had provided the spectacles like lightening-in-a-bottle that wowed seventeenth-century publics, and Charcot's use of the camera enabled his fans to "see" insanity, the *moving*-picture camera put a new means of amazement into the hands of science's aficionados in the early twentieth century. "Seeing evolution," writes Clark, was made possible by running a succession of photographs through a "moving picture machine," the idea for which was likely inspired by the movie *Evolution* circulating in theaters at the time. According to Clark, "Visualizations like [*Evolution*]—or the existence of movies in general, and the acute awareness of moving pictures as a way of seeing—affected the way people, including scientists, conceived of evolution."[29]

The "Great War" as Spectacle: When Casualties Become Story-Telling Props

In their edited volume *War as Spectacle*, classics scholars Anastasia Bakogianni and Valerie Hope depart from the conventional historical studies of wars as military events, and the cultural studies of wars' representations for their impact on the way we understand our present. Rather, they consider war as a form of performance, war *as* spectacle. In their "theoretical model," as they put it, "war becomes a type of theatre, a spectacle performed for the benefit of an audience." In the ancient world, they tell us, "war was used as entertainment ... and violence was a means for grabbing the audience's attention."[30]

In his chapter for the Bakogianni and Hope book, Tobias Myers tells us that war becomes spectacle when "it becomes the object of viewing for characters within the story." He uses the duel between Paris and Melelaus in *Iliad* 3 to illustrate the ancient interplay between performers and those watching. The duel is staged as a proxy for the war between the Trojans and Achaens. Prior to the duel commencing, the armies have been disarmed and recast by Homer as spectators to the event. Helen as well, has been invited as "audience." Myers describes the effect of the spectacle:

> By casting his work as a spectacle and elaborating on the audience, the poet also makes [his] work more of a draw. A cat caught in a tree might catch one's eye, but a cat in a tree surrounded by a crowd is almost irresistible: one is impelled to stare at what everyone else seems to find so interesting, and also to gawk at the other onlookers. In the case of the duel, the extra interest generated by a multitude of watchers is not without a certain irony. In place of the expected bloodshed, deaths, and derring-do on the large scale ... the war has been reduced to its bare, unglorious essentials.[31]

Later in *War as Spectacle*, Justine McConnel argues that the nineteenth century was "an era of spectacle *par excellence*" in which classical literature, war, and theater were brought together. The element of spectacle in Victorian burlesque and French operetta, according to the author, was also "attested to in other forms of entertainment of the day, indicating audiences' great appetite for novelty and visual extravaganza." As we've seen, it was that same cultural milieu—classical paintings, theater, new technology (photography) and audience enchantments with modern science—that nurtured the diagnostic breakthroughs now associated with Jean-Martin Charcot's work at Salpêtrière.[32]

A seedy variety of the spectacle-healing culture, known as Mountebank or quackery in Europe, manifested in the early twentieth-century America as the traveling medicine-shows staged on horse-drawn wagons pulled from town to town. Audiences were drawn to the shows by carnival barkers who introduced preforming acrobats and other entertainers while promising the yet-to-appear "doctor" who would reveal the healing powers of this or that elixir.[33] The attractiveness of the entertainment–science confections peddled by these charlatans made it an avatar of the traditional–modern mix that had animated scientific advancement for several centuries. And, flashing forward, it anticipated the public's vulnerability to the greatest-yet "staging" of violence waged with new and exotic technology in which the actors themselves provided the images through which the event would be known and remembered: World War I. The war's massive killing by the modernist marvels of long-range artillery, aircraft, and poison gases was an obscenity, itself a spectacle beyond previous comprehension. And yet from within, there appeared a second-order spectacle, that of paralytic bodies, veterans whose curious afflictions were made by motion-picture magic into the images through which the war-as-spectacle would be remembered.

The best studies we have linking the historical legacy of spectacle, science, and war trauma are those of German film that were inspired by World War I. In his book *Shell Shock Cinema: Weimar Culture and The Wounds of War*, Anton Kaes reminds us that interest in "nerves" and nervous disorders arose in the late nineteenth century out of concern about modernization and urbanization. Charcot's work had left a residue that associated nervousness with weakness and femininity so that, when Kaiser Wilhelm predicted in 1910 that the coming war would be won by the side with the strongest nerves, he effectively equated psychological and emotional tolerance of violence with masculinity and martial prowess.[34]

It followed, then, that the first casualties of what came to be called shellshock presented medically with distorted body postures that mimicked those of Charcot's female patients, images that had been popularized through mass media and, in turn which, attributed veterans' maladies to insufficient masculinity, or femininity. That possibility raised, as well, questions about the effect on doctors of *their* acculturation to the legacy of Charcot: was it possible that feedback loops connecting doctor–patient expectations influenced what doctors were looking for and found?

It would be years before the interplays of spectacle, medical science, gender, and war trauma which had been tangled by the cultural environment of the early twentieth century would be approached critically. Twenty-first-century information technology and social media enabled a melding of combat-performance and audience that was never imagined during the Great War. US ground troops with cellphone cameras recorded themselves urinating on dead Iraqi soldiers and staging tortures at Abu Ghraib prison, many with sexual inferences. Their self-recorded atrocities went live to audiences at home, bypassing the scrutiny of military and civilian authorities. Seen by critics, the homophobic and misogynist imagery sent pridefully across the Internet by young men in Iraq was symptomatic of a wounded masculinity cradled in the American post-Vietnam War culture, wounds that would metastasize into a vindictive political movement during the twenty teens.[35]

In the meantime, scholars delved into the ways that Germany's loss in World War I and Italy's frustrations with post-war settlements generated anxieties for which entertaining spectacles, accompanied by promises to deliver miracle solutions, were the salve. The wake of the war that was the spectacle-of-all-spectacles merged entertainment media with political propaganda to create the spectacular extravagances that were the hallmark of fascism leading to World War II.[36]

Fascist Spectacle: Italy. In her *Fascist Spectacle: The Aesthetics of Power in Mussolini's Italy*, Simonetta Falasca-Zamponi argues that Benito Mussolini, also known as *Il Duce* or the leader, viewed the public masses as an aesthetic phenomenon to be shaped and molded, sculpted, by the hands of political leaders *cum* artists. The domination of the "masses" by female qualities such as feebleness and irrationality, as he thought the case to be, meant that women were incapable of art, including the art of politics. Thereby, Mussolini held the "masses" to be incapable of self-governance or democracy, casting the lot of leadership to strong and virile men.[37]

With politics thusly aestheticized, Mussolini saw "the mass-object's feminine status" as a condition of primal irrationality that could be politically mobilized by appeals to "faith, myth, and cults." The idea that the "masses" could be moved by images, words, and feelings," says Falasca-Zamponi, "led Mussolini to adopt a political style that privileged the symbolic aspects of power relations, the mystical side." "By beautifying politics," in this way, she writes, "fascism reaffirmed the value of tradition—a tradition founded on hierarchy and respect for authority …" Mussolini also made mass participation an element of the very human–mass–object he was sculpting into political form. "The 'masses' were at the same time," according to Falasca-Zamponi, "part of the fascist spectacle *and* fascism's spectatorship; they were acted upon and actors."[38]

The subject–object dialectic that made the "masses" the spectacles of their own consumption played out most memorably in the mass rallies researched by the sociologist Gustave LeBon for his classic study of crowd behavior, *The Crowd: A Study of the Popular Mind*. As identified by him, the characteristics of the crowd included "impulsiveness, irritability, incapacity to reason, the absence of judgement … [and] the exaggeration of sentiments." They were the same attributes he ascribed to "inferior forms of evolution," that is, as Falasca-Zamponi commented, "women, savages, and children."[39]

Violence, however, extended wartime's spectacle-of-spectacles into the fascist period, and in keeping with the previously identified fusions of traditional and modern-enlightenment spectacles that enthralled public gatherings, fascists employed violence against pacifists and socialists for no other reason than their victim's opposition to violence. "It was in the nature of the movement's own dead," writes Falasca-Zamponi, "that fascism claimed its legitimate role in determining the future of the Italian nation."

> By magnifying the fascists' blood and sacrifice, the regime sanctified violence as the premise for Italy's renewal ... In its idealized and exaggerated form, the cult of the fallen ... bloomed during the regime.[40]

The fascist myth of the Italian nation, however, imagined it as an internally undifferentiated and conflict-free mass society. It was an image that required a distorted public representation of fascist violence that *diminished* the number of its victims and *exaggerated* the numbers of fascist martyrs. Falasca-Zamponi calls the fascist violence "a self-absorbed experience" that eventually had to internationalize itself in the form of a unified nation at war with an external enemy.[41]

Mussolini's attraction to a mythical Italian nationalism was nourished by the legacy of the Roman Empire, perhaps the architype of global empire. The architectural ruins of the Empire's monuments to greatness lay strewn about modern Italy as reminders of what it once was, and an inspiration to The Duce to imagine what it could be again. Viewing architecture as a form of spectacle that could move the masses, he set about building futuristic roadways, new sports stadia, and an entire new district of Rome.

Grand as his designs were, though, they were no match for the architectural extravaganzas that Adolph Hitler's megalomania was raising in Germany, gargantuan works of steel and stone intended to ignite the passions he needed for the cult of blood and death that was forming.

Fascist Spectacle: Germany. Hitler experienced World War I as a soldier. Wounded and temporally blinded in a British gas attack, he had convalesced in a military hospital in Pomerania. While there, he grieved the loss of the war and conceived the ideas that "weakness" in the national will-to-war and "invisible foes" had cost Germany its victory. To some extent, those were overlapping causes and, in any case, the "will" to root-out the treachery and duplicity embodied by the Jews, Communists, and other enemies of fascism would require a tolerance for mass violence that he saw lacking.

"What the masses needed," [Hitler] thought,

> were ... symbols that would win their faith, pageantry and color that would arouse them, and acts of violence and terror which, if successful, would attract adherents (were not Germans drawn to the strong?) and give them a sense of power over the weak.[42]

Hitler's sense of "the weak" was, like Mussolini's, a feminized notion that took shape in his mind as a reaction to the emancipatory themes of the Weimar Republic that had followed the First World War. The Weimar constitution of 1919 had given women the right to vote and granted equity in marriage and civic affairs. Eighteen years later, Heimrich Himmler, who managed the Nazi concentration camps, declared (with an ironic choice of words) that "we have too much masculinized our life":

> For me, it is a catastrophe that women's organizations, women's communities and women's societies intervene in a domain that destroys all feminine charm, all the feminine majesty and grace. For me, it is a catastrophe that we ... want to make women an instrument of logical thought, to educate them in everything possible, that we want to masculinize with time the difference between the sexes ... We must be very clear ... [That] ideology cannot be sustained if it is worn by women, because man conceives of everything through the mind, whereas women grasp everything through sentiment.[43]

Hitler aspired as a young man to be an artist and was reportedly frustrated to have been rejected from art school before the war. He painted, nevertheless, and critics to the present remain divided about the quality of his work, and there is no evidence for an aesthetic impulse in his politics as is seen in Mussolini. But Hitler's adoption of the hakenkreuz, or swastika, as the symbol for the Nazi party that would "arouse" the populous to carry out the unspeakable, as William Shirer put it, revealed his sense for the power that an image "as old, almost, as man on the planet" must have: An artist's intuition, perhaps, but additional evidence for an understanding of spectacles as amalgams of epoch-blending symbolism.[44]

With visions of architectural grandeur that surpassed those of Mussolini, Hitler designated the architect Albert Speer to create them. In his memoir *Inside the Third Reich,* written while he was incarcerated in Spandau Prison for his World War II crimes, Speer ruminated on his own Duce-like fantasies that the ruins of the past could, as they did for Mussolini, imbue the nation with the idea of modern empire. "Our architectural works," he thought at the time, the early 1930s, "should also speak to the conscience of a future nation centuries from now." From that, Speer evolved his "Theory of Ruin Value" that the buildings and monuments of empire had to leave evidence of their greatness for hundreds, even thousands, of years that their ruins would evince. Speer took his "theory" to Hitler who bought into it.[45]

Speer's first major assignment from Hitler was to build a podium for Nazi party rallies on the Zepplelin Field at Nuremburg. Zepplein Field was named for the airships that Germany had weaponized for World War I and based at the field. The Party had held annual rallies since its formation in 1923 and sometimes used the field. But after his appointment as Chancellor in January 1933, Hitler wanted something more than the wooden stands that occupied the space. Speer proposed replacing the wooden structure with a permanent stone edifice that was 1,300 feet long and 80 feet high. Inspired by the Pergamum alter in near Pergamum in Asia Minor, it was twice the length of the Baths of Caracalla in Rome, and featured "a mighty flight of stairs topped and enclosed by a long colonnade flanked on both ends by stone abutments."[46]

Speer added lights and color to the party rallies giving them the touches needed to make them the spectacles they are remembered as. He rescheduled the events for nighttime and ordered 130 spotlights to light up the sky and illuminate the banners and flags carried by local party groups, giving them, in his words, "an element of surrealistic surprise." "The actual effect," he wrote, "surpassed anything I had imagined: The hundred and thirty sharply defined beams, placed around the field at intervals of forty feet, were visible to a height of twenty to twenty-five thousand feet, after which they merged into a general glow. The feeling was of a vast room, with the beams serving as mighty pillars of infinitely high outer walls ... I imagine that this `cathedral of light' was the first luminescent architecture of its type ... and after its type, the only one which has survived the passage of time."[47]

The Zeppelin Field project was only the first of Speer's efforts to satisfy Hitler's megalomania, with the New Reich Chancellery and German pavilion for the 1937 world's fair in Paris to follow. And by that time, the spectacle value of the field was already surpassed by the political violence that would end in the death camps that defined the Holocaust.

Hitler promised to be the Fuehrer who could bring the weakness and decay of post-Weimar Germany to a Final Solution. The vanguard for fulfillment of the promise would be the World War I veterans seeking vengeance for the home-front betrayal they held responsible for their defeat. Rather than disarm after the war, they assembled into a militia known as the Freikorps, for Free Army. Wearing discarded brown Army shirts—in imitation of Mussolini's black-shirted shock troops—they had terrorized Weimar loyalists and opponents of the war since the November 1918 Armistice. By 1931 this "band of fanatical and ruthless men" had rallied to Hitler as the S.A. or Strumabteilung, or storm troopers, who were, recalled Shirer, "with increasing frequency, taking to the streets to molest and murder their political opponents."

Seeing Mussolini having come to power through coups and seeing the grip that he held on the Italian people using the bloodshed of martyred fascists to fire demands for vengeance, Hitler used the same violence-begets-violence calculus to leverage his own rise to power. The Nazis found their own *martyr célèbre* in Horst Wessel, a young fascist militant killed by the communists in 1930, in what Shirer called "the street wars." Before his death, Wessel had written a song that would become an anthem of the Third Reich. Sung to the tune of the Christian hymn *How Great Thou Art*, the opening lyrics of the Wessel song read:

Flag high, ranks closed,
The S.A. marches with silent solid steps.
Comrades shot by the red front and reaction
March in spirit with us in our ranks.
The street free for the brown battalions,
The street free for the Storm Troopers.

Millions, full of hope, look up at the swastika;
The day breaks for freedom and for bread.[48]

The martyred Wessel may have been the poetic muse of Germany's fascist movement, but the humiliation of the lost war and the hardships imposed by the Treaty of Versailles fueled the vengeful sentiments of its mass social base of support. The second line of the song's third stanza, "The time of bondage will last but a little while now!" referred to the subservience that people felt themselves subject to and the commitment of the Nazi party to free them of the stigma. The signature martyrs of the movement were the dead and wounded war veterans. Victimized by bad leadership and betrayed by broad swaths of civilians, as the Freikorps thought the case to be, the dead had paid the ultimate price for national weakness, and the still-paying living-wounded were visible symbols of the national hurts that cried out for redressing.

The most moving images of war-veteran victimization were the paralytic, sometimes mute or blind, and traumatized veterans who presented socially as proxies for the collective trauma that the nation continued to suffer. Metaphors for the public impotence and shame that the war left behind, the shellshocked veterans provided the spectacle that the fascists made into propaganda tools to rekindle the emotional fires for war.

Analogies are always imperfect and likening America's post-Vietnam War funk to Germany's interwar despair is no exception. But President George W. Bush's declaration at the end of the Persian Gulf conflict that we had "kicked the Vietnam Syndrome" left little doubt that it was the loss of the *last* war that had revved the war machine for the new war.

The Gulf War experience also witnessed the president appealing for public support, making the means-of-war, the soldiers sent to fight it, the reason *for* the war. Characteristic of traditional sentiment, the appeal prioritized the flesh-and-blood commitment of soldiers over that of abstract notions of, for example, democracy and free markets. The soldier-centered appeal was juiced by claims that Vietnam veterans had been disparaged by the antiwar community and we wouldn't do that again. Support for the troops sent to the Gulf spawned a yellow-ribbon campaign, a spectacular repudiation of the Vietnam-era betrayals held responsible for the defeat in Southeast Asia.

The specter of Vietnam played strongly enough in American imaginations during the Gulf War to cement a lost-war culture reminiscent of Europe's interwar revanchism. The following chapters will show the role played by war casualties that whet the German appetite for more war, and how the American post-Vietnam War cultural trajectory retraced that path. Latter iterations of victim-veteran imagery in medical literature and popular culture set the stage for MAGA's appearance.

Notes

1 Bensaude-Vincent and Blondel, *Science and Spectacle in the European Enlightenment*, 2.
2 Bakogianni and Hope, *War as Spectacle*, 10.
3 The French psychiatrist was Jean Martin Charcot whose work discussed in greater detail later. Beginning in 1951, NBC aired "Mr. Wizard," a science program for children. Mr. Wizard was performed by Don Herbert, pointedly described by *Smithsonian Magazine* as "an educator who loved spectacle as much as he loved science." Mr. Wizard was the inspiration for *Bill Nye The Science Guy* that aired decades later. Read more: www.smithsonianmag.com/smithsonian-institution/meet-mr-wizard-science-guy-inspired-bill-nye-180956371/#ADTA7lyiotQ732pm.99
4 Zeitlin, *Ideology and the Development of Social Theory*, 216–221.
5 Bensaude-Vincent and Blondel, 7.
6 Ibid., 8.
7 Scott, *The Politics of Readjustment*, 252.
8 http://catalogue.museogalileo.it/room/RoomXI.html
9 Simon in Bensaude-Vincent and Blondel, 145, 151–152 provides a detailed description of the dissection and fluid injections involved in Fragonard's preparation of human corpses for his work.
10 Ibid., 145, 151.
11 Some of the models are preserved at Musee Fragonard, Ecole veteriaire, Maisons-Alfort. Simon, 154 in Bensaude-Vincent and Blondel.
12 Traditionalism's uppercase T connotes its identity as a school of thought, a philosophical orientation.
13 Shephard, *A War of Nerves*, 15–16.
14 Erichsen, *Railway and Other Injuries of the Nervous System*, 73.
15 Charcot published 61 case histories of male hysteria, cases which Showalter says were "crucial to understanding the construction of masculinity ..." Those writings remained obscure, however, because they were not translated into English until the 1990s, a delay in time that allowed hysteria in war veterans to be hidden under euphemisms such as shellshock and post-traumatic stress disorder.
16 Gilman, *Seeing the Insane*, 6.
17 Ibid., 28.
18 Showalter, *Hysteries*, 34.
19 Ibid., 31–32. The former student quoted by Showalter was Pierre Janet.
20 Ibid., 32, notes Charcot's interest in debunking the church's "miracle cures." Showalter, 34, elaborates the socio-economic conditions that accounted for many of Charcot's patients being working-class women.
21 Ibid., 164.
22 Browne, *Darwin and the Face of Madness*, 158 opines that psychiatric photography was popular in part because of "the attractions of the art of photography itself ..." Gillman, Ibid., 716–717 wrote of "... facial expression as an infallible indicator of psychological states."
23 The results of Charcot's use of photography may also have presaged recognition of "the Hawthorne Effect," the alteration of a research environment by the research process itself. Coincidentally (perhaps), the studies at the Hawthorne factory giving rise to that concept in the 1920s were conducted by Elton Mayo who according to Martin Stone, *Shellshock and the Psychologists*, 248, began his career as a "shellshock doctor with Australian army."
24 Showalter, *Hysteries*, 36.
25 "Warped celebrity" is Showalter's phrase, Ibid., 36–37. Showalter cites Leon Daudet's *Les Morticoles* as a "savage novel [that] portrayed Charcot as the sinister Doctor Foutange who manipulates his patients like a puppeteer." Roth in "Science Odyssey" says the

resemblance between the poses struck by Charcot's patients and classical paintings was "not an accident."

26 Shephard, *War of Nerves*, 98 recalls that Herman Oppenheim in Germany believed that shelling created microscopic lesions in the brain and nervous system, causing the paralysis seen in veterans. Although Oppenheim's idea was soon discredited, according to Shephard, 99, it would be resurrected in the early 2000s for a successor to shellshock, traumatic brain injury (TBI). For an August 12, 2012 *New York Times* column "War Wounds," Nicholas Kristoff wrote about Iraq War veteran Ben Richards who is being treated for PTSD/TBI, reporting that lesions have been found in his brain.

27 Shephard, *War of Nerves*, 98. As late as 2013, the search for "biomarkers," something physical that could be connected to PTSD, was ongoing (see Dao, 2013). O'Sullivan, *Sleeping Beauties*, 177 writes about psychosomatic illness as being a type of its own, an irreducible whole greater than the sum of its mind–body parts. However, she adds a third part "societal pressure," that can "create a medical drive to explain disorder[s] in a biological way to mitigate against its social implications." Categories of war trauma from shellshock through PTSD and its derivatives illustrate her point.

28 Gilman, *Seeing the Insane*, 204.

29 Clark, *God or Gorilla*, 159–60.

30 Bakogianni and Hope, *War as Spectacle*, 2–5.

31 Ibid., 33–34. Myers (in Bakogianni and Hope, 25) says oral and written forms of storytelling are made spectacles when listeners are induced "to 'see' with the mind's eye."

32 In Bakogianni and Hope, Ibid., 257–269, see McConnell "Eric Parodies: Martial Extravaganzas on the Nineteenth-Century Stage." The nineteenth-century wars referred to by McConnell were the Crimean and Napoleonic.

33 See Corey Dolgon, *Kill It to Save It* for more on medicine shows.

34 Kaes, *Shell Shock Cinema*, 39.

35 Ford and Hoskins, *Radical War*. The theme of wounded masculinity will be developed in subsequent chapters.

36 Dipple, *War and Sex*, discusses the crisis of Western masculinity fostered by the women's' movements around the turn of the twentieth century.

37 Falusca-Zamponi, *Fascist Spectacle*, 23–25. The author uses the form: the "masses."

38 Ibid., 25, references Walter Benjamin for "anesthetized politics." The italicized emphasis is added.

39 Ibid., 18.

40 Ibid., 36.

41 Ibid., 37–40.

42 Shirer, 42.

43 Longerich, *Heinrich Himmler*, 234.

44 See Shirer, *Rise and Fall of the Third Reich*, 43 on the swastika and Schyeldahl, *Hitler as Artist* on the 2002 exhibit of Hitler's painting at the Williams College Museum of Art.

45 Speer, *Inside the Third Reich*, 66.

46 Ibid., 65. Wikipedia describes the Pergamum Alter as "a monumental construction built on a terrace of the acropolis near the ancient city of Pergamum." The Baths of Caracalla in Rome, built in AD 212–217 covered 62 acres and required 2,000 tons of material every day for six years.

47 Ibid., 69.

48 Shirer, *Rise and Fall of the Third Reich*, 147. The authorship of the Wessel song is contested. For more on the song see www.anesi.com/east/horstw.htm

2

SHELLSHOCK

Political Culture, Medical Minds, and Moving Pictures

> The double wound of war and defeat festered beneath the glittering surface of its anxious modernity. The Nazis exploited that shameful memory and mobilized the nation for another war to avenge the first.
>
> (Anton Kaes, *Shellshock Cinema*)[1]

Robert Gerwarth's book *The Vanquished: Why the First World War Failed to End* was reviewed by Margaret MacMillan in *The New York Times* Sunday Book Review on December 11, 2016. In her review, MacMillan, a historian of international history, quoted the German war hero Ernest Junger as writing in 1928, "this war is not the end but the beginning of violence." Junger's view, MacMillan wrote, was aligned with those of other Europeans who welcomed violence as an ennobling way to "degrade their enemies while creating new societies." The public embrace of violence that Junger witnessed was, as well, a facet of the fascist extension of war-as-spectacle into the civil life of the interwar period that was described in Chapter 1.[2]

Catapult to More War: Germany's Dolchstosslegend

The most dramatic instance in which the loss of a war and its costs in human lives and limbs were used to justify more war occurred in Germany after its defeat in World War I. Throughout the war, the German people had endured enormous suffering. Food shortages and other deprivations, suffered unevenly by rich and poor on the home front, added to the pain of human losses in the war. Though the war had begun to go badly by the spring of 1917, the German leadership continued to assure the people that victory was in sight. A soldiers' mutiny in June

DOI: 10.4324/9781003391906-3

1917 and a string of strikes in early 1918 notwithstanding, the German people continued to sacrifice while the government tried to suppress dissent. When the end finally came late in 1918, the German people felt, with considerable reason, that they had been misled. Why, they wanted to know, had they been asked to sacrifice so much in a losing cause.

Leaders of Imperial Germany such as Gen. Erich Ludendorff and Field Marshall Paul von Hindenburg deflected this anger by blaming opponents of the war and supporters of the Weimar Republic for having betrayed the German cause. The Weimar Republic, which was Germany's first attempt to establish constitutional democracy, replaced imperial rule after World War I and was under attack by German rightists from the start. These anti-Weimar forces converged with other reactionary elements after World War I to form the fascist movement leading to the triumph of the Nationalist Socialist Party and the rise of Adolf Hitler to power in 1933.

During World War I, Hitler had gained notoriety for his oratory against Jews, Marxists, and other "invisible foes" who he said would deny the German people their victory. While recuperating from a war wound, he found "scoundrels" cursing the war and wishing for its quick end. "Slackers abounded," Hitler wrote, "and who were they but Jews."[3] To ground the idea that German soldiers had been betrayed on the home front, the German right promulgated three images that combined to evoke powerful, even primal sentiments, that were then manipulated for political purposes: the idea of war veterans being abused when they returned home; the gendering of the betrayal narrative for an indictment of women and "the feminine" in the culture; the use of Shellshock imagery as a metaphor for the German nation traumatized by the lost war and in need of rehabilitation through rearmament and the vindication that victory in another war would bring.

The Myth of the Hostile Homecoming: Gendered and Medicalized

It was German propagandist Hermann Goering who promulgated the idea that "very young boys, degenerate deserters, and prostitutes tore the insignia off our best front-line soldiers and spat on their field-gray uniforms." Goering would later gain infamy as founder of Hitler's security police, known as the Gestapo, and his description of veterans' homecomings became "a fanatical belief ... which more than anything else, was to undermine the Weimar Republic and pave the way for Hitler's triumph."[4] But Goering, wrote journalist William Shirer in *The Rise and Fall of the Third Reich*, was mythmaking.

Most German soldiers returned rather quietly from the war and made the transition to civilian life without fanfare or fuss. Goering's claim that some had their insignia ripped from their uniforms has some basis in the fact that, as the war was ending and it was clear that Germany had lost, thousands of soldiers were in revolt against their officers. In acts of defiance against the authority of the old regime, and to express their solidarity with a left-wing revolutionary movement that was growing across the land, soldiers ripped the insignia from the uniforms of their own officers.[5] So *some* German soldiers were attacked—those officers. But the detail that the attackers were themselves uniformed soldiers was left out of Goering's rendition, and it subsequently became lost in the *Dolchstosslegend*, the legend of German soldiers stabbed in the back, their military mission betrayed on the home front.[6]

Much of what we know about the German stab-in-the-back legend comes, not from these rebel veterans, but from the diaries, novels, and poems written by veterans who became members of the Freikorps. The Freikorps was a paramilitary movement that sought to avenge what it alleged had been the betrayal of German troops on the home front. Freikorps literature often portrayed "the enemy" as female–female with male anatomical and sexual powers. Freikorps fiction writers sometimes represented the traitor as a proletarian woman with a pistol hidden beneath her skirt. For his 1987 book *Male Fantasies*, historian Klaus Theweleit studied those stories and was struck by their Freudian character. The imagined pistol, Theweleit said, was an expression of male fears of a female with male power, a female with a penis; the women described by Freikorpsmen as spitters, he said, was a fantasy of women with the power to project a body fluid.

In *Die Geachteten*, Freikorps member Ernest Salomon described an antimilitary demonstration against the Berthold Freikorps in Hamburg:

Shaking their fists, the women shriek at us. Stones, pots, fragments begin to fly … They hammer into us, hefty women dressed in blue, their aprons soaked and skirts muddied, red and wrinkled faces hissing beneath wind-whipped hair, with sticks and stones, pipes and dishes. They spit, swear, shriek … Women are the worst. Men fight with their fists, but women also spit and swear—you can't just plant your first into their pusses.[7]

Writing in the preface for Theweleit's book, the historian and scholar of women's studies Barbara Ehrenreich explained that male fears of female bodies arose from the primal depths of the unconscious:

The dread arises in the pre-Oedipal struggle of the fledging self, before there is even an ego to sort out the objects of desire and the odds of getting there: It is a dread, ultimately of dissolution—of being swallowed, engulfed, and annihilated. Women's bodies are the holes, swamps, pits of muck that can engulf.

It was a fantasy so threatening, concluded Theweleit that it had to be annihilated.

The gendering of the betrayal narrative in this way evinced the same psychological forces that Falasca-Zamponi found at work in the formation of Italian fascism (see Chapter 1). The association of national defeat with weakness that was then feminized and cast as home-front duplicity eased the evolution of the narrative into the shellshock imagery that animated Germany's lost-war revanchism, propelling it into a new war.

Spun as a kind of war-wound inflicted on veterans, the myth of home-front hostility was easily fused with the medical discourse entering public conversation as the new diagnostic category, shellshock. And just as retrospective studies of Charcot's work at Salpêtrière pointed to the influence of art and culture on what the patients were exhibiting and the doctor was seeing, reviews of shellshock's origins see it cradled in the popular culture of the times. Writing in *A War of Nerves*, historian Ben Shephard calls shellshock an example of "a common modern phenomenon: a medical debate, hedged with scientific qualifications, taken up by public opinion and the media in an oversimplified way."[8]

Doctors, in the early twentieth century were, themselves, not impervious to the influence of popular culture; and photography, still new in medical use, had the power of spectacle. Charcot's photographs had made their way into the public realm where they were particularly popular among doctors. That chain of influence sketches a feedback-loop running from the doctors in the asylum where the photographs were taken, through the public's fascination with them after their appearance in popular publications, and back to doctors working in the hospitals in the following years. In his 1985 essay "Shellshock and the Psychologists," historian Martin Stone wrote of the early war period that, "Shellshock had, it seemed, caught both the sympathy and imagination of the public who [in turn] 'raised the psychoneuroses to the dignity of a new disease before which doctors seemed well-nigh helpless.'" In short form, these scholarly assessments suggest that art and photography, if not having led science in the making of the diagnostic category known as shellshock, were powerful influences.[9]

The *gendered* threads of shellshock are also traceable through the connection of art to psychiatric diagnosis but in this case the threads get a twist. The utility of the shellshock diagnosis was cultural as much as medical because it diverted the search for the cause of symptoms away from causes with sex or gender implications. The idea that the symptoms observed could be due to fear of either bodily injury or failure was objectionable because it linked, in the minds of psychiatrists, to hysteria which led in turn to the photographic images left by Londe's camera—which were women—and the paintings in Charcot's clinic that prompted Londe's subjects—which were paintings of women. Those graphic images formed a paradigmatic barrier to the ability of the doctors to follow a train of thought leading to either psychological or socio-cultural explanations for the symptoms they observed—put sardonically: *anything but psychological.*[10]

Ironies abound, however, in the studies of how shellshock came to grip the imagination of the public and the medical profession. On the one hand, attempts to account for the symptoms were leaden with popular impressions of the military technology associated with them that bent the search away from psychological explanations. On the other hand, the nature of those very technologies had within it the characteristics that kindled psychological imaginings—imaginings that ran in some minds to conspiratorial plots to deceive the public and undermine the military mission.

The Great War in Triple Spectacle: Machines, Their Casualties, and Moving Pictures

The "War of Machines." Called the War of Machines in some accounts, one of The Great War's most spectacular sights was that of exploding shells that cast plumbs of gravel and dirt into the air that then rained down upon soldiers hunkered in trenches. Known as the "buried alive syndrome," the fear of being trapped under mounds of debris was one of the early conditions associated with shellshock. The sounds, too, were of a war never before experienced. Civilians in East Sussex, England across the English Channel and many miles from the front were reported to have heard the sounds of the big guns firing in France. With sights and sounds of that magnitude impressing on peoples' senses of the war, there is little wonder that thoughts about its casualties, even those that appeared to be mental or emotional, were thought of in physiological terms.[11]

The Unseen Incoming from the Big Guns

Artillery was nothing new by 1914. The use of gunpowder to throw large objects long distances dates from twelfth-century China and soon thereafter the technology spread across the Middle East and Europe. The power of the guns increased steadily between the fourteenth and eighteenth centuries, as did their accuracy and mobility. After a centuries-long experimental phase, explosive shells, distinct from solid-shot cannon balls, debuted as the benchmark of modern artillery. The prototypes featured bombs with fuses that were lighted as they exited the gun muzzles. In 1784, the British artillery officer Henry Shrapnel invented a timed fuse for shells which was the innovation that defined modern artillery weaponry going forward.

Advances in the machine-tooling of gun barrels, known as "rifling," increased the accuracy and velocity of the fired shells, but by the time of the US Civil War their maximum range was still about 300 yards. In a 2017 YouTube video clip demonstrating the capacity of Civil War guns, we can see the smoke and vapor of the gun's discharge 3–4 seconds before the explosive impact of the shell.[12] By World War I, however, the range of artillery guns had increased to a distance that put them well beyond sight of the enemy. The 75 mm field gun with which the French began the war, for example, had a range of three to six miles, while the German "Big Bertha" howitzer ranged beyond seven miles. By the end of the war, Germany had developed the so-called Paris Gun that had a range of 75 miles, a capacity that put their discharges out of sight *and* sound of the allies on the receiving end.[13]

The out-of-sight-ness of enemy firepower added a stealth quality to its dangers. With no forewarnings of the explosions that were about to occur, soldiers already stressed by the squalid conditions of their trenches now had the terrifying anxiety of their own deaths to live with—in a sense, making the *unknown* the greatest-known enemy. Even when heard, the sound of the guns added more to the horror of the experience than the enhancement of protective measures. Writing about the effects of the long-range, fast-loading artillery, historian Adam Hochschild quoted a British officer's recollection of a German attack:

> Louder and louder grew the sound of the guns … under a sky of brass, shaking with the concussion of artillery, now a single heavy discharge, then a pulsation of the entire atmosphere, as if all the gods in heaven were beating drums the size of lakes.

The unpredictability of the big guns' dreadfulness inflicted psychological damage on its human targets that would be more lasting than the reparable material damage left by the explosive shells themselves. It would be hard to quantify *stealth* but whatever the shock to neural and emotional systems left by the sheer terror of unannounced death or dismemberment left by the anticipated incoming of conventional explosives, it must have been immeasurably increased by the poison gases that could be delivered by the same guns.

Death, Brought to you by the Wind. The modern technologies that moved the death-delivering cannon miles from their victims also enhanced their immunity to retaliation—How could the enemy strike back against what it could not see? In a sense, long-range artillery redefined the meaning of combat, diminishing the romanticism associated with *mano-a-mano* confrontations like those staged by the ancient Greeks on which traditional masculinity depended. The tarnishing of combat's aura by the remoteness of artillery was augmented with shells that took battlefront stealth to a higher and even more terrifying level: chemical warfare. "Now," wrote Hochschild, "with deadly gas brought to you not from the hand of an enemy you could see and slay, but the very wind, all bravery seemed useless."[14]

The first gas used was chlorine by the British at the battle at Loos on September 25, 1915. The gas was stored in canisters that were hand-carried to the front by British soldiers and then sprayed toward the German trenches. But chlorine was defended against by face-covering gas masks with which the Germans were supplied. Some of the gas blew back on the British and the rest settled to the ground across which the British troops attacked only to then be contaminated—by their own gas. "All told," Hochschild found, "the British suffered more casualties from their own gas than the Germans."[15]

Mustard gas was the most common and debilitating chemical compound weaponized for the war. First used by the German's in July 1917, it was a colorless gas that sometimes took on a yellow tint and mustard-grass smell when prepared for military use. The German's deployed it by artillery, their own gunners kept safe from it by their distance from their targets; by 1918, a third to a fifth of all artillery shells were filled with gas.[16] The gas was heavier than air so it hugged the ground upon impact and dipped into the trenches—the very defenses against artillery that were emblematic of the war; it also leached into the ground from where its contamination continued to spread by ground water and wind.

The breathing apparatuses devised to protect the lungs from gases like chlorine left clothing and skin exposed to Mustard's painful blistering effects.
Shephard describes the effects of Mustard gas:

> To see a flesh-and-blood human being, your comrade perhaps, mutate into a slimy creature—"the white eyes writhing in his face," "the blood ... gargling from the froth-corrupted lungs"—was a terrible experience, bringing to the surface fundamental fears ... Foul air entering the throat arouses in everyone a primitive fear of being choked or asphyxiated and triggers the instincts of self-preservation which go with it.

It was the capacity of gasses to silently seep and linger undetected that lent them a reputation as a stealthy killer. "Gas," Shephard concludes, "was—and has remained—as much a psychological as a physical weapon."[17]

Nothing says Stealth like a Submarine. Soldiers stricken with the disorder known as shellshock commonly presented the symptoms of anxiety, nervous tics, and insomnia, conditions they attributed to the uncertainties and prolonged periods of apprehension they had endured at the front. Hunkered in trenches for weeks and wondering the whole time, when will the next artillery shell burst, with no warning, just feet away from them? Or when might the usual morning mist creeping toward them turn out to be a lethal gas?

Civilians in London, New York, or even Berlin who might have been able to imagine the terror experienced by their respective kin and kind in uniform, were pulled even deeper into the reality of wartime fear when the British passenger ship RMS Lusitania was torpedoed by a German submarine off the coast of Ireland on May 7, 1915, killing 1,198 passengers. Civilians exempted from military service for reasons of gender, age, or ability who could have *only* imagined being under bombardment in a trench were now forced to reconsider their own insulation from the war. They, or family and friends who might have been on *that* Lusitania could well be on the next.

Historians of the war's mental health impact suggest that the paranoia spawned by its surreptitious tactics—the out-of-sight artillery and obscure gases—lived on in the unsettled psyches of its veterans, along with the physical disabilities they carried. But the broader post-war societal cultures that strummed the conspiratorial chords of fascism in Germany and Italy as well as anti-Axis apprehensions elsewhere were undoubtedly amplified by the haunting could-have-been-me stories told by civilians and merchant marines of trips taken, or not, through sub-infested waters.

The terror of German submarines running deep and silent in Atlantic waters is best remembered in allied accounts for its impact above the surface on the sailors and passengers onboard British and American ships. But the German sailors *on* the submarines themselves may have been in even greater danger. Over half of the German submarines, known as U-boats, were sunk by the end of the war. According to a BBC historical site, of the 17,000 men who served on the boats, 5,100 died, making it one of the war's most dangerous assignments.[18]

It was hiddenness of the death-makers below the water line that preoccupied the public memories of WWI going forward but the hazards of crossing the Atlantic had been increased by the unseen killers aboard—the munitions being secreted to the British by the Yanks. The Lusitania went down with 128 Americans, few of them aware that the ship also carried tons of munitions that, when struck by the German torpedoes, was what set off the explosion that sent the cruise ship to bottom within minutes.

The battles of WWI waged on the high seas was a Stealth vs. Stealth closed circle in which the trans-Atlantic smuggling of armaments called forth the furtive German submarine tactics that brought still added unseen dangers to the human-kind involved both below and above the surface.

That it was the covert undertow of long-range artillery, chemical warfare, and submarine sneakery that produced the visual and imaginary spectacles of shell-blasted earthen geysers, blistered human flesh, and exploding ocean liners through which WWI would be represented is ironic, in a way. The war was, after all, billed as the War to End All Wars, modernism's triumph over tribal traditionalism and the ignorance of the pre-rational world—the cultural milieu in which spectacle held the stage. In retrospect, though, we know that the war's spectacles birthed as much myth and legend as any war. And, as is the case with things phantasmagorical, it was the liminality of its own story lines—it's stealth technology and no-man's-lands that bred ghostly legends about unaccounted for MIAs—that left public moods unsettled after the Armistice of November 1918. It was the war's *unknowns* that haunted its memory and fed fascinations of what had *really* happened. And nothing fired those imaginations more easily than the causalities, living and dead, that the war had created.[19]

The Casualties. The combination of men and machines so symbolic of the war also catalyzed a medical approach to casualties that renewed interest in "railway spine," a paradigm that placed the cause of disorders outside the mind and body of the patient, and, thereby, privileged physical symptoms such as paralysis as a "man's malady." A gendered bias inherited from the nineteenth century, it easily transferred its diagnostic prejudices to use in treating war causalities.[20]

British doctor Dr. Henry Head believed that men under fire in the trenches had to suppress their instinct to survive by running away; the body then converted that fight-or-flee conflict into a paralysis of the legs, a condition recognized as a "symptom" that could justify a soldier's removal from danger.[21] Others speculated that paralysis was a positioning-in-place of arms and legs that fixed them as they were at the time of exposure to explosions—sort of like bracing for the impact of a train collision. Indeed, the exaggerated concave back positioning presented by some shellshock patients may have been imitations of railway spine (or female hysterics) seen by veterans in films or newspapers. Like the paralysis of a limb, other forms of immobility such as dumbness or insensitivity to stimuli were thought by William Rivers to be reassertions of instincts dormant since earlier stages of human evolution, vestigial responses to danger calling for silence and stillness.[22]

It was the British doctor, Charles Meyers who put the term shellshock into vernacular use. Meyers was seeing soldiers who suffered from tics and tremors, some gone blind or deaf, others paralyzed; many showed no signs of *physical* injury. It was a puzzling combination of medical facts: bodies appearing to be otherwise healthy were behaving in abnormal ways. Meyers speculated that these patients' behaviors were due to exploding shells on the front, their conditions the result of the invisible energy shock emitted by the explosions.

But then, soldiers who had yet to see combat appeared with similar symptoms. In Germany, soldiers who had never been under fire were more likely to present symptoms than those who had. The Freiburg physician Alfred Hauptmann reasoned that soldiers with actual physical wounds should exhibit shellshock symptoms— but they seldom did. Moreover, he thought, if shell explosions did directly cause neuroses, then soldiers would surely suffer these symptoms from firing their own weapons, a phenomenon that he had never observed."[23] Dr. Joseph Babinski reasoned the symptoms may be "brought about not by the war itself but either by unintentional suggestion from doctors or by the patient's auto-suggestion and imitation"[24]—words that cue for us the that doctors at the time were considering that emotions, psychology, and perhaps culture were factors in the symptomology of shellshock.

With shellshock embedded, as it was, in the public imagination, wrote historian J.C. Dunn, "the "lurid journalese of home [news]papers" … prepared the minds of the draft[ees] for receptivity to suggestions that they would soon be suffering suffer from it." Or, in the words of Doctor William Johnson who had studied as a neurologist, won commendation for bravery at the battle of the Somme, and later treated war casualties, "Young soldiers prepare to become a case of shellshock almost before the first shell drops near them."[25]

Freudians suggested that shellshock patients had repressed the conflict between fear and duty, and what the patient was *really* afraid of was his own failure. The repressed memories of failure later reemerged as fantasies of the military accomplishments they thought were expected of them—false memories, but replete with the physical symptoms attributable to combat—and *conjured* exploding shells.[26,27] Historian Michael Roth says shellshock in many ways resembled hysteria, a kind of "body speak,"—the bodily reappearance of ideas, fears, maybe even memories banished from consciousness.[28] But hysteria was a female disorder. Doctors, wrote historian Elaine Showalter, were, "so prejudiced against a psychological cause that they just kept looking and looking"—some kind of wound on the body, evidence of a bomb blast, something physical. Anything but psychological.[29]

The doctors were men schooled in the tradition of the neurologist Jean-Martin Charcot who had a theory that hysteria was caused by "brain lesions." The theory had been largely discredited in his day when autopsies failed to reveal the lesions, but it had a manly anything-but-psychological character that nevertheless led to its resurrection for approaches to WWI casualties. Borrowing Charcot's idea, Herman Oppenheim in Germany believed that exploding shells created microscopic lesions in the brain causing paralysis. Conceivably, this model fit the gender-driven imperative that the causes of male nervous disorders could not lie within the man himself: the lesions theory put the cause, exploding shells, outside the patient; the exploding shells, in turn, conjured the combat bona fides of the victim; and the damage was physical—a robust model for sure.[30] But Oppenheim had to admit that the sought-for lesions were "too small to be detectable." Historian Ben Shepard in *War of Nerves* noted that Oppenheim's lesions-model was "comprehensively routed" even before the end of the war.[31]

The Moving Pictures. Historians' wide agreement that camera photography influenced Charcot's analysis of women hysterics suggests that modern medical science is as susceptible to the impressions of visual spectacle as was its predecessors. That part of what went on at Salpêtrière lends support for the idea that doctors believed not just what they could see, but the visuals they could document. The new diagnostic category called forth by the presentation of *paralysis* beckoned a new spectacle-making technology and the *moving*-picture camera was just what the doctors ordered.

On the face of it, the mustering of moving-picture technology seemed simple enough. The photographs and film footage of the war's mechanical marvels, even without their assaults on the senses of front-line fighters, would seem to have produced visuals enough to make medical sense of the casualties. But Anton Kaes in his 2010 book *Shellshock Cinema: Weimar Culture and the Wounds of War* points out the paradox that so much of the war actually took place out of sight. The part of the war responsible for shellshock was, he says:

> difficult to capture on film because much of it took place underground, in rat-infested, muddy trenches, where hundreds of men lay hidden from view, waiting for weeks to be attack or be attacked. "To be seen dead"—this slogan epitomizes the aporia for visual media in the first all-out technological war.

To be seen dead, or even paralyzed, was to bring to the public mind's eye, bring to *life*, in a sense, the realness that the greatest spectacle of the war's spectacles was actually its quiet and invisible terrors—and moving pictures of war veterans who could not move were its visual documentations.

As if to validate the observation made by historians that the popular awe of "science" in the sixteenth century was induced by showmen appearing to have captured lightening in a jar, and that Charcot had called-forth the shimmies and shakes he wanted his audience to interpret as symptoms by dressing his patient–performers in hats and long feathers, early film itself repeated the drill. There was a synergy, Kaes suggests, between early film itself—jumpy, with abrupt juxtapositions, and silent—and the symptoms it purported to capture—spastic movements, contortions, and muteness. A century later it is easy to imagine that the oddness of body images appearing in these big-screen prototypes when seen for the first time by young men, perhaps even before the war years, suggested that certain postures and movements carried mental health implications—perhaps even elicitations of "look how crazy that guy in the movie looks!"[32]

The certainty that film was another instance of the *medium being the method*—not just the message—to the same degree that Londe's photographs shaped the construction of hysteria cannot be established, of course. But Kaes is certain that the post-war cinematic representation of World War I veterans as victims of shellshock was an essential element of political culture, especially in inter-war Germany. The 1920 German film *The Cabinet of Dr. Caligari*, for example, was one of the first and most influential films of a style known as expressionism that sought to represent fears and ambiguities laying otherwise unacknowledged at some deeper level of consciousness. In *Caligari*, the character Cesare is a veteran representing the horrors of the war he carries into Germany's future. Cesare appears early in the film standing, but inanimate, in an open and upright coffin. Haltingly, under the influence of the mysterious Dr. Caligari, Cesare begins to move. He steps from the coffin in the stiff and jump-cut motion resembling the recovering shellshock victims in film footage later spliced into documentary films that virtually define shellshock for us.[33]

Kaes's blunt identification of the real-life Charcot as the model for the filmic Dr. Caligari, and his suggestion that Cesare might have been case number 365, as recorded in a 1919 medical collection called *Shellshock and Other Neuropsychiatric Problems*,[34] fills in a matrix of mutually influencing relationships in medicine that ranged across the years: doctor–patient interactions, developments in communication technology from photography to film, the mutual influences of modern warfare with media representations of medical and military events, and the role of artistry (painters, photographers, screenwriters) in the creativity of medical science, shaping as they moved over the years, public memory of wars past and imaginations of wars to come.[35]

Movies were so new to so many people in the early 1920s that they were a spectacle as a form of entertainment media, in and of themselves. Regardless of *what* was projected on the screen they represented to audiences the epitome of modernism, a harbinger, even, of the future. Like with scientific advances of the past—and a scientific marvel they surely were—their attractiveness to mass audiences was enhanced when joined with imagery that evoked the unresolved anxieties stemming from unsettled pasts. And so it was, that it was the scary surrealism of *Caligari*'s scenes—cockeyed buildings, disconnected pathways— in which we see disturbed-looking characters that might have walked out of Charcot's asylum that proved irresistible to viewers.

The film's first spoken line tells us, "Es gibt Geister ... uberall sind sie um uns her." Kaes translates the line as "There are ghosts ... all around us" and interprets the German *Geister* to mean also "phantoms," "apparitions," or "specters." Explaining the reference to Geister, he writes:

> [It] places the film in a pre-cinematic tradition dating back to the ghost shows and phantasmagorias in which spirits were made to rise from the dead in a dark room—spectacles produced by the optical illusions of a magic lantern ... Although most of the phantasmagorical shows pretended to give a scientific explanation for their technologically produced apparitions, they nevertheless produced moments of simulated madness in which the supernatural intruded into the rational world. Such, of course, is cinema, and Weimar cinema in particular.[36]

The most epistemic effect of shellshock cinema was, however, that it completed the subject–object loop by which victim-veterans who had once been the *means* of the Great War's violence became through filmic representation, subject-agents implicated in the creation of the shellshock label that would define them, and still later the consequential *ends* that would come to define what the war and its loss were all about. They had been, in effect, made into spectacles, the *visual* manifestations of the unseen spectacles of stealth warfare and props for the construction of post-war narratives that led to more war.

Hidden Injuries: The Political Text

The political effect of shellshock imagery in German culture was studied by Siegfried Kracauer for his 1947 book *From Caligari to Hitler*. Films like *Caligari*, he said, used the medical imagery of shellshock to suggest to Germans that the loss of the war had also been a social and cultural shock to their pride and national identity. The wounded Germany symbolized by the shellshocked Cesare in *Caligari* had been betrayed on the home front by pacifists, Communists, women, and Jews. The grounding-image of the sell-out was the stabbed-in-the-back German veteran, spat on when he returned home, his uniform shed in shame at the rail station lest it be ripped from him by the traitors. Metaphorically, shellshock was the unseen wound carried by veterans, and the body politic as well, as the silent disease of national trauma demanding vengeance through more war.

Shellshock's intrigue synced with public anxiety about the unseen dark sides to the technologies thrust upon them by the war. The spectacular sights and sounds of the great war machines accounted for the physical damage—material and human—left behind, and the invisible nature of other wounds hid still more dangerous social and political unknowns. The stealth-character of long-range artillery, submarines, and toxic gasses fueled the proto-paranoia of an evolving betrayal narrative for Germany's loss and a reassessment of what losses in war meant, even for the victors.

The "Gold Star Mother": The Spectacle of Death as an Achievement

The United States had not entered the war formally until April 1917 and did not send troops until June of that year. Its combat losses of 53,000 dead and missing were enormous for the seventeen months of its involvement, but less than 10% of the total losses taken by the Allied powers. Conventional historical accounts of the American post-war years remember the national triumphalism that fed a rapacious consumerism, the "flapper" music and dance crazes that dominated the cultural scene, and the business expansions that branded the decade as the "Roaring 20s."

Beneath the celebratory veneer, however, controversies lingered over the war, some of which mirrored those that hung over Europe. US entry to the war had been opposed by left-wing working-class movements like the Industrial Workers of the World, many of whose members were foreign born. The Russian Revolution of October 1918 and a raft of worker revolts that swept Germany as the war ended emboldened still greater militancy: in Seattle, workers mounted a February 1919 general strike and in July the Communist Party USA was formed.

A victor in the war, the United States was not subject to the revanchism that swept post-war Germany and Italy. Bitterness against pacifists, strikers, and a rising feminist movement, however, nourished a reactionary climate with long-term implications. Along with pacifists and anti-draft organizations led by Jane Adams and other feminists, and labor reform groups such as the IWW (Industrial Workers of the World), also known as the Wobblies, were attacked as subversive threats to national security. Attorney General A. Mitchel Palmer launched a roundup of foreign-born activists for deportation in late 1919 and early 1920. The paranoia surrounding the anti-Red campaign, known historically as "The Palmer Raids," was not so dissimilar to the betrayal-panic then engulfing German and Italy.

Almost simultaneously with the founding of the American Communist Party in 1919, war veterans formed into the American Legion. Not quite a German Freikorps replication, the Legion nevertheless announced its violent identity on Armistice Day 1919 by raiding the IWW hall in Centralia, Washington and lynching Wesley Everest who was in the building. Throughout the 1920s, the Legion supported compensation for veterans, opposed educational materials it deemed un-American, and advanced ultra-nationalist views.

Losses such as the United States did suffer in World War I, worked as they did in Germany, to galvanize a stronger sense of national identity. In her 2010 book

Bodies of War, Lisa Budreau refers to the American "cult of the fallen soldier" produced by the war, which she said provided "justification for the nation in whose name the war had been fought." "The notion of heroic death was readily invoked," she wrote, "to assuage the grief of the living while furthering the interests of the nation."[37]

The American institution of "Gold Star Mothers" was born in this Post WWI social climate. The traditional black adornments signifying grief and mourning were supplemented by gold stars that counterbalanced funereal symbolism—a gold star for accomplishment, writes Budreau sardonically. A *New York Times* editorial on the gold-star concept claimed that, "There is no better death than this."[38]

Images of nineteen-year-olds lying dead in Vietnam, soldiers bringing the war home with them as "hidden injuries" of trauma, and veterans disparaged by pacifists and radicals as villains in an unpopular war revivified the "cult of the fallen soldier" in American imagination in the years after the US defeat in Vietnam. In a magnitude beyond what even Siegfried Kracauer might have thought to be likely 30 years hence from his 1947 writing of *From Caligari to Hitler,* the mainstream news media and Hollywood film made Vietnam veterans into political props for slandering the antiwar movement and whetting a popular vindictiveness for the lost war that could only be satiated by more war.

But post-war cultures are many-layered things. At first blush, there seems to be a straight line from the period of reaction that followed the First World War— police raids on radical centers, the formation of a right-wing veterans' group, and the cooptation of grief for political purposes—to President Ronald Reagan's 1980 declaration of the war in Vietnam as "a noble cause" and President George H. W. Bush's effort to "shake the Vietnam Syndrome" by sending troops to the Persian Gulf in 1990. But cultural history is seldom a straight line.

By the 1930s, artists in New York and Hollywood working in the mold of German expressionism were bringing to theater and literature the disturbing images and storylines hanging over from America's stint in the war. For his 1936 play *Bury the Dead,* Irwin Shaw used zombies, ala *Caligari,* to represent the psychological discomforts that go on after the shooting stops. In the play, six US soldiers killed in the war refuse "orders" from military officers to stay buried and accept the honor of having died gloriously—as scripted by the reigning nationalist sentiment that Budreau describes in *Bodies of War.* Instead, the walking-dead use their "visits" to authorities and relatives to remind their countrymen of war's futility, their persistence to live a metaphor for the unsettled conscience of a nation that has gone to war without good cause. For his 1938 novel *Johnny Got His Gun* Dalton Trumbo created the World War I veteran Joe who had lost all his limbs, senses, and face in an artillery explosion. Joe's mind is fine, though, and by tapping Morse code with his head, he manages to tell the world the class realities of modern war.

Trumbo's "Joe" and Shaw's ghostly nightwalkers are casualties of the war as certainly as the shellshocked figures that animated Germany's interwar propaganda and the gloriously dead doughboys commemorated by their Gold Star Mothers— but they strike very different political postures. Joe and Shaw's veterans refuse to be seen as victims, choosing instead to recast themselves as warriors against the wars they had fought, allies in the struggle for peace rather than losses to be avenged through more war.

Antiwar warriors or victim-veterans? As the former, Vietnam veterans were a threat to the pro-military establishment seeking to shake public reluctance for another go at war abroad, while the latter image had more political ambiguity. Pacifists could spin the victim imagery as costs-of-war that were too great to pay (again), while the political right could leverage it, in the way shellshock casualties were used by German fascists, to scapegoat the domestic peace movement for having added to soldiers' risk by opposing the war effort, and to avenge the societal hurts, represented by the wounded, through more war.

We know now that the question of how Vietnam veterans would be represented and remembered would drive a campaign to psychologize the image of antiwar veterans through the construction of the new diagnostic category post-traumatic stress disorder. Chapter 3 will show the way news media and film made antiwar veterans into spectacles, enlisting them in a propaganda campaign that disparaged them as victims and degraded their political integrity.

Notes

1 Kaes, *Shellshock Cinema*, 2.
2 MacMillan, "Neither War Nor Peace" p. 16 *New York Times* December 11, p. 16.
3 Shirer, *Rise and Fall of the Third Reich*, 30–31.
4 Hamilton, *Who Voted for Hitler*, 334; Ibid., 31.
5 De Jong, *Weimar Chronicles*, 15.
6 Instances of US officers attacked by their own men are similarly forgotten in the popular remembrances of the war in Vietnam. Many Americans seem to "know" that GIs were mistreated upon their return from the war, but lost in the myth that veterans were spat on by protesters is the history of "fragging," the practice of solders killing their own officers.
7 Theweleit, *Women, Floods, Bodies, History*, 65.
8 Shephard, *War of Nerves*, 58–59.
9 Browne, *Darwin and the Face of Madness* 158; Stone, *Shellshock and the Psychologists*, 254.
10 The details of World War I battlefront realities provided by Reid, *Broken Men*, 58–70, make it understandable that doctors and military authorities had a hard time sorting out cases of malingering, self-mutilation, hysteria, and imitation from actual shellshock—which itself was still an emergent concept.
11 The 2011 film *War Horse* set in World War I provides a dramatic contrast between the old horse-drawn technology that began the war and the twentieth-century machines that brought it to an end. The skills of horsemanship and hand-wielded weaponry like sabers were no match for artillery and tanks. The mechanization of war, moreover, proletarianized the armies, reducing skilled fighters to little more than bodies in the trenches, the life or death of which provided a means of measuring the productivity of the machines.

12 The YouTube video is here: www.youtube.com/watch?v=jL1DkrYL70s
13 For the specifications of the French guns, see: www.passioncompassion1418.com/decouvertes/english_fusees_artillerie.html#hautpage. On Big Bertha, see: https://en.wikipedia.org/wiki/Big_Bertha_(howitzer).
14 Hochschild, *To End All Wars*.
15 Ibid., 163.
16 Shephard, *War of Nerves*, 63.
17 Ibid., 63. His description of dying from Mustard appears to be taken from Harris and Paxman *A Higher Form of Killing*, 24–25.
18 See www.bbc.co.uk/guides/zq3q2hv
19 H.G. Wells is credited with having called WWI "The War to End Wars" in 1914.
20 Young, *The Harmony of Illusions*, 41, captures the power of railway spine to frame doctors' thinking on war causalities: "A half-century after the publication of Erichen's first book on railway accidents, [World War I] physicians ... were witnesses to an epidemic of traumatic paralyses, contractures, anesthesias, and aboulias ... as if a hundred colossal railway smashups were taking place every day." Anesthesias, contractures, and aboulias are all associated with difficulty in moving. In Caruth, *Unclaimed Experiences*, 16, we can see the presence of the railway spine studies in Freud's thinking.
21 Head may or may not have recognized that the soldier's evacuation as a casualty also extricated him from the moral dilemmas of war, while satisfying as well the societal standard for masculinity—a wounded veteran is a *combat* veteran.
22 Hunters are familiar with the ability of animals, like rabbits, to sit motionless in order to disguise their whereabouts. If evolutionary development has programmed a startle response into humankind, it's as likely to be the instinct to "sit" when threatened, writes psychologist Susan Cain, as to more actively engage the danger.
23 Shepard, *A War of Nerves*, 106, 112; Hochschild, *To End All Wars*, 199, describes gunners that "bled from the ears after five days of nonstop firing."
24 Ibid., 11–12, 98.
25 Dunn, *The War the Infantry Knew*, 250; Johnson is quoted by Shephard, *A War of Nerves*, 58–59.
26 Harrington, *The Cure Within*, 75–76, has an accessible account of Freud's breakthrough. See also Stone, *Shellshock*, 255, for the reworking of Freud's insights by British psychologist W.H. Rivers. *New York Times* columnist Maureen Dowd, in her May 22, 2010 column "Wishes as Lies," made clever use of Freud's insight in writing about Connecticut Attorney General Richard Blumenthal's false claim to being a Vietnam veteran.
27 W.H. Rivers' insight would be reprised by Hyer et al. for a 1990 study that found low self-esteem rooted in parental practices was a better predictor of suicide among Vietnam veterans than was military experience.
28 Roth's words are quoted from the 1998 PBS documentary *Odyssey of the Mind* which featured Freudian orientations toward Shellshock in the years after WWI.
29 Showalter, *Odyssey of the Mind*.
30 Shephard, *A War of Nerves*, 98. The histories of war-trauma diagnoses are laced with issues of masculinity. Dipple, *War and Sex*, explores those issues as a prelude to World War I itself.
31 Shephard, *A War of Nerves*, 99.
32 Tellingly, the soundless property of early film correlated with muteness (and deafness), and complimentarily, with the absence of the startle-response presented by veterans of later wars who claimed that a sharp and unexpected noise like a firecracker caused them to relive wartime experience. In "Flashbacks ... and Firecrackers" I wrote about the properties of those stories as legends. It was a symptom that would be closely associated with PTSD after the war in Vietnam—and well after sound was married to

motion pictures in the 1930s. Chute, *Disaster Drawn*, 86–89 suggests the relationship between film and representations of trauma.

33 *Caligari* was written by Hans Janowitz and Carl Mayer and directed by Robert Wiene.

34 Southhard, *Shellshock and Other Neuropsychiatric Problems.*

35 Kaes, *Shellshock Cinema*, 66, says Cesare might have been case number 365, as recorded in a 1919 medical collection called *Shell Shock and Other Neuropsychiatric Problems Presented in 589 Case Histories from the War Literature, 1914–1918.* Whether Cesare's herky-jerky motions are performed by the actor Conrad Veidt, or are an artifact of the film's jumpy quality, they can be compared with documentary images of shellshock patients seen in the 1998 PBS *Science Odyssey.*

36 Kaes, Ibid., 55.

37 Budreau, *Bodies of War*, 4, 44.

38 Ibid., 95–97.

3

THE SPECTACLE OF ANTIWAR WARRIORS

Political Dissent Is Made a Medical Disorder

> A vet escaped from the Brentwood VA ... [Psychiatrist Leonard] Neff rushed to the scene and called out to him, "Attention! This is Captain Neff. The mission is accomplished. You don't have to fight anymore. Lay down your arms." The vet surrendered peacefully.[1]

> Colonel Trautman: "The mission is over, Rambo. You understand me? The mission is over ... It's over Johnny."[2]

Post-traumatic stress disorder (PTSD) is "Exhibit A" for the case that diagnostic categories can be manufactured by social and political forces outside of medical science, and that those forces are powered by spectacles having little to do with medicine. It was Vietnam War veterans with long hair and necklaced love beads, marching arm-and-arm with protesters to end the war from which they had just returned, that turned the heads of all Americans—a spectacle indeed. But the figures of warriors-against-the-war would have their most historical impact on healthcare professionals.

News reports exaggerating the radicalism of veteran dissent; stories with photographs of eccentric clothing or placards; reporters and editors making references to the mental and emotional conditions of veterans based on their behavioral and bodily expressions—all the practices criticized by Sander Gilman's in *Seeing the Insane* cited in Chapter 2. It was the synergy between street politics and news media that began the rewriting of the Vietnam veteran coming-home experience to a mental health discourse from its profoundly political beginnings.

The imperative to psychologize the storyline of Vietnam veterans derived from the political dynamics of the Moratorium Days against the war in 1969.

DOI: 10.4324/9781003391906-4

Designated as days when business-as-usual would stop for teaching and reflecting on the war, the first Moratorium Day, October 15, was a huge success. Thousands of Americans who had not previously taken a public stance turned out for antiwar events. The success of the day signaled to the Republican presidential administration of Richard Nixon that opposition to the war was reaching into middle America. In response, the administration launched a political attack intended to divide the radicals in the movement from its newly emergent liberal wing. By deploying a rhetoric of betrayal—those who are opposing the war are betraying the fighting men in Vietnam—the administration hoped to discourage the continuation of mainstream America's involvement in protest politics.[3]

Sir! No Sir![4]

The problem with the administration's strategy was that by 1969, thousands of Vietnam veterans were, themselves, part of the antiwar movement, and hundreds of men still in the service were openly opposing the war. Green Beret Sergeant Donald Duncan had been the cover-page portrait for the antiwar magazine *Ramparts* in February 1966. Duncan had "quit" the military after witnessing atrocities committed against Vietnamese. Although he said in an interview for the 2006 film *Sir! No Sir!* that he was unaware of any antiwar movement,[5] the movement had already established a reputation for its support for draft resistance and service to military members resisting from inside military organizations. With the imprimatur of Duncan and other in-uniform dissenters, a group of civil-liberties lawyers in New York City reported a "great jump" in the number of clients on active duty who were refusing to carry out military orders in Vietnam.[6] The first major case involving support for in-service resistors was that of the "Fort Hood Three." Ordered to report to the Oakland Army Terminal on July 13, 1966, for shipment to Vietnam, three Army enlisted men stationed at Fort Hood, Texas refused to go. While on leave prior to their reporting date, they traveled to New York City to seek support for their action. On their way to a public meeting at the Community Church in New York City, they were abducted by federal agents and taken to the stockade at Fort Dix, New Jersey where they were court-martialed and sentenced to two years in prison. Subsequent demonstrations on their behalf helped focus the attention of the antiwar movement on GI rights.

As the antiwar movement was reaching out to help military personnel, soldiers lent their voices to the movement. The archives of antiwar organizations contain scores of letters and petitions recording the widespread support of GIs for the movement. They began coming in long before the peak of campus protest activity in 1968 and 1969 and took unexpected forms. One, found in the files of the Fifth Avenue Peace Parade Committee, was signed by George J. Bojarski and 14 other members of an infantry platoon in Vietnam. Sent to the mayor of Dearborn, Michigan, Orville Hubbard, the letter expressed support for a referendum on the war that the mayor had placed on the ballot for the November 8, 1966, election, and their gratitude that the vote had gone against the war.[7]

Links between veterans and the antiwar movement deepened on April 15, 1967, when Vietnam Veterans Against the War (VVAW) announced itself at a large rally in New York City. For the next two years the organization provided speakers for public events, ran newspaper ads against the war, and published its own newspaper, *Vietnam GI.* In 1968, a group within VVAW supported Democratic Party antiwar candidate Eugene McCarthy's nomination for president and led efforts to actively organize in-service GIs for resistance to the war. The April 1969 mobilizations against the war, known as the Easter GI-Civilian Demonstrations, raised the demand to free protesting soldiers held in the Presidio stockade in San Francisco, and notched up GI organizing to a new level. For the first time, organizers gained access to the New York City Port Authority bus terminal, enabling them to pass out leaflets and talk to GIs passing through the terminal, a central transfer point for GIs moving across the mid-Atlantic region.

Discrediting Antiwar Veterans: *Not Really Veterans, Not Real Men*

The success of the October 15 Moratorium startled even the planners. In New York and Boston over 100,000 people turned out to protest the war. The October 24 issue of *Life* magazine called it "a display without historical parallel, the largest expression of public dissent ever seen in this country." And the Moratorium spirit carried to Vietnam's battle zones where *The New York Times* reported that members of a platoon of the American Division wore black armbands in support of the stateside protest.

The magnitude of the civilian–military collaboration was alarming to the Nixon Administration and its response was to challenge the credibility of these antiwar warriors. Initially, that challenge took the form of raising questions about their authenticity. Administration spokesmen would plant doubt about the identity of protesting veterans by making statements to the press such as, "We've been unable to confirm how many of the self-identified veterans at the demonstration really were veterans." Or they would question the masculinity of radical veterans with gay-baiting remarks. In one of his speeches, Vice President Spiro Agnew joked that he heard one protesting veteran tell another, "If you're arrested, give only your name, address, and telephone number of your hairdresser."[8] The administration also infiltrated VVAW to build a legal case against it. That effort resulted in the court case known as "The Gainesville 8," in which VVAW members were charged with conspiring to terrorize the 1972 Republican National Convention in Miami Beach, Florida. The "eight" were acquitted, and the course of the trial revealed that it was Richard Nixon's "plumbers," later convicted for crimes related to the Watergate case, who had infiltrated VVAW with agent provocateurs and attempted to incite the veterans to commit violence.[9]

If dissident veterans couldn't be dismissed as inauthentic or "not real men," their credibility could be impugned in another way, by raising doubts about their mental stability. Ultimately, this is the course of events that led to the establishment of a new psychiatric diagnostic category, PTSD, which would marginalize the voices of antiwar veterans for decades to come.

Psychologizing the Political

The use of psychiatric labels to stigmatize unwelcomed social behavior has a long history in Western medicine.[10] In Vietnam, disciplinary problems were sometimes "medicalized" and treated as psychiatric casualties. In his 1970 book *Men, Stress, and Vietnam*, Army psychiatrist Peter Bourne wrote that commanding officers "very often … suggested to the psychiatrist that a psychiatric evacuation would be a very acceptable way of removing a troublemaker from their unit."[11] The most famous example of this is probably Charlie Clements' case.[12] Clements graduated second in his class at the Air Force Academy in 1969. After flying a few missions in Vietnam, he refused more assignments on the grounds that he opposed the war. His superiors sent him for psychiatric evaluation which led to his confinement in a military mental hospital in Florida. Following his release from the military, he graduated from medical school and in the 1980s became famous for founding the organization Medical Aid to El Salvador.

The extension of psychiatric labeling to cover the political behavior of dissident Vietnam veterans came about through the convergence of efforts by mental health professionals and journalists. Since 1969, a small group of psychiatrists had been working to formulate a new diagnostic concept that would apply to soldiers psychologically hurt by the war. A decade later, their efforts would bear fruit with the inclusion of PTSD in the psychiatric profession's *Diagnostic and Statistical Manual (DSM)*. But in the early 1970s, these psychiatrists were having difficulty finding a receptive audience for their concept, then called post-Vietnam syndrome (PVS).

The legitimation of war trauma as a psychiatric ailment was dogged by the same sort of empirical issues that challenged the veracity of shellshock—recall from Chapter 2, those shellshock patients who were never exposed to exploding shells. The psychiatrist Peter Bourne reported objective comparisons of urinary 17-OHCS levels, the adrenal secretion associated with stress, for combat and noncombat troops. Tests of helicopter medivac crews showed no higher rates of 17-OHCS on days they had taken hostile fire than normal, and actual higher rates on nonflying days than flying.[13] Bourne's finding may have surprised many readers but, for those who knew the field, it would fit comfortably with data from World War I.[14] As was the case by 1970, however, controversies over how the war has being fought, and lost, were intensifying with pro- and antiwar sides loading their rhetoric with references to veterans' experience: hawkish conservatives spinning opposition to the war as being hostile to the men who were still fighting it; dovish liberals citing the dangers facing troops as a reason to stop the war, and denouncing as demagoguery the support-the-war-because-the-troops-are-there rhetoric coming from the right.[15] As time went on, both sides sought enhanced leverage through the infusion of mental health narratives into their positions: hostility to soldiers and veterans was a form of betrayal with emotional psychological consequences, said one side, while the other pointed to the mental and emotional costs that accompanied the loss of arms, legs, and lives in combat.

Political Spectacle Makes the News, the News Makes Medical Science

As if cued by Martin Stone's revelation (Chapter 1) that it was the irresistible newspaper imagery of veterans disturbed by their war service that moved WWI-era doctors to adopt the framing of shellshock, it was news coverage of the veterans' 1972 protest of the Republican national convention that moved Vietnam-era doctors to adopt a mental health framing for what they were seeing.

The August convention in Miami Beach, Florida was originally scheduled for San Diego, California, but the protests and police riot that had scuttled the Democratic Party convention in Chicago four year earlier, and the intensity of the antiwar demonstrations that had closed colleges and universities in 1970 after the US invasion of Cambodia, led Republican planners to relocate: Miami Beach's moat-like perimeter would be easier to secure. The decision to move a major political convention in order to manage political dissent was remarkable enough; and yet it would be an editorial decision made by *The New York Times* made on the same day that would change medical history in ways consequential for the national political culture for decades to come.

On May 6, 1972 the *Times* ran an op-ed piece written by Dr. Chaim Shatan. In it, the psychiatrist argued for adoption of diagnostic nomenclature covering what was still called PVS at the time—and it was the same article the *Times* had rejected 15 months earlier. During those intervening months, however, caravans of antiwar veterans and their supporters had converged on the Capitol grounds in Washington, D.C. where they camped for days while lobbying in the halls of Congress to end the war. On April 22, 1971, the fourth day of the camp-in, John Kerry then a spokesman for VVAW, delivered a denunciation of the war before a congressional committee now recognized by some as one of the great speeches of the twentieth century. The next day, hundreds of veterans marched to the Capitol steps where they tossed over a fence their medals awarded for service in Vietnam. Photographs and footage of those defiant acts became some of the most iconic images of the war years—spectacles of Americanism turn upside-down in which we see the once-heroic executors of national foreign policy now in militant opposition to it.

The veterans' incursion into the belly of establishment power rattled the nerves of policymakers. Rusty Lindley who had been a military advisor in Vietnam remained in Washington after the VVAW event to continue the lobbying effort to end the war. Advisors to President Nixon and leaders of the Veterans Administration, he later told sociologist Wilbur Scott, vowed to not let dissenting veterans "affect public support for the war."[16] Even in those first days following the camp-in, the Nixon schemers began imagining a strategy to discredit the veteran political voice by casting it publicly as a symptom of wounded emotions; those high-level ruminations got their call-to-service a year later as the Republican convention approached.

With interest in the political impact of anti-Vietnam mobilizations rising, Shatan, the psychiatrist, suggested to the *New York Times* in May of 1972 that "it was an opportune time" for the publication of his essay; the *Times* agreed, and the piece appeared on May 6.[17] After that, Shatan told Wilbur Scott, "The telephone began jumping off the wall ... things started mushrooming." A round of public forums and academic conferences followed, laying down the path to the professional adoption of the war trauma terminology, PTSD, in the 1980 DSM. That it was the political dynamics playing out in the streets and halls of Congress that had enhanced the timeliness of new thinking on war trauma—not a change in the scientific credibility of the PVS terminology proposed by Shatan— confirms what the historians of science cited in Chapter 2 have known to be the case for centuries.

The *New York Times*'s endorsement of Shatan's idea was clearly the game changer in the history of American discourse on war trauma. But two other sets of events played important ancillary roles: the *Times*'s coverage of the veterans' demonstration at the upcoming Republican convention, and the film industry, for having already excited the imaginations that led the scientific thinking on the disorder to begin with, and then, as in interwar Germany, for casting war trauma in the political narrative of national betrayal.

The *New York Times* Medicalizes Veteran Dissent

As it should have, the *Times* reported on the extraordinary occurrence at the Republican convention of war veterans in the street to protest the war they had been sent to fight. And given the legitimation the paper had recently given to the notion of a post-Vietnam syndrome, there was no surprise when it spun the VVAW action as a mental health story. On the very day the convention opened with over a thousand protesting veterans in the streets, the *Times* ran a front-page story, above the fold, with the headline "Postwar Shock Is Found to Beset Veterans Returning from the War in Vietnam." The article was accompanied by a three-column-wide photograph of a single GI dragging his duffle bag down an airport hallway. Behind him on a wall is a large banner reading, "Welcome Home Soldier. USA is proud of YOU." The irony of the forlorn soldier brilliantly juxtaposed against the sentiment of the banner is inescapable.[18]

The continuation of the story on the inside was set off with an eight-column-wide repeat of the headline and a different photograph showing a lone veteran sitting head-in-hand, slumped over a chair at the Oakland, California army terminal. The caption described him as "weary" and then continued with the allegation that 50% of Vietnam veterans needed "professional help to readjust."[19] The association with mental illness was deepened in the text of the story that contained a liberal sprinkling of phrases like "psychiatric casualty," "emotionally disturbed," "mental breakdowns," and "men with damaged brains." The story provided no data to support the portrait of dysfunctional veterans that it painted; what it did provide was a mode of discourse within which America's memory of the war and the veterans' coming home experience would be constructed.

On the second day, 1300 Vietnam veterans led by three disabled veterans in wheelchairs conducted a silent march to the Republican Party headquarters at the Fontainebleau Hotel. There, Ron Kovic, a leader of the march who became the basis for the movie *Born on the Fourth of July*, addressed himself to the delegates assembled. Barry Romo, a leader of VVAW, raised objections to Nixon's plan to turn the war over to the South Vietnamese saying, "Veterans want an end to the war, not a change in the color of the skins of those who are dying."[20]

The "Crazy Vet" Movies

If PTSD was as much the construction of journalists as psychiatrists, it was not fashioned from materials found solely within the veteran population. The clues for what PTSD was made from can be found in the literature of shellshock pointing to the nineteenth-century photographs of hysterical women that fed back into medical culture to later jump-start the scientific minds imagining a post-Vietnam descent of shellshock. As an antecedent to the sequencing of visual arts and the conceptualization of PTSD, the semblance of shellshock's trajectory is obvious.

The public image of Vietnam veterans was pathologized by Hollywood almost from the outset. After a brief spate of films that fitted characters home from Vietnam into the storylines typical of post-World War II innocence—veterans with no adjustment problems reentering their hometowns with happy families and welcoming employers[21]—the mood changed. "Joe Corey" in the 1965 *Blood of Ghastly Horror*" is a brain-damaged veteran with an electronic implant that makes him prone to homicidal fits. In the same year," Brahmin" in *Motor Psycho* suffers psychological trauma from the war; lapsing into delirious recollections of fighting the Viet Cong, he rapes and kills before being taken down.

Black Sunday. Political veterans, such as those assembled in Miami Beach in 1972, had cameo big-screen appearances in *Greetings* (1968), *Getting Straight* (1970), and *The Revolutionary* (1970), but deranged and dangerous remained the stock representations of veterans going forward from there. The first major Hollywood contribution to PTSD imagery came with *Black Sunday* in 1977. In it, a veteran unhinged by his experience in Vietnam, commandeers the Goodyear Blimp on behalf of a Palestinian terrorist group. He arms the blimp with plastic explosives intending to fly it on Super Bowl Sunday over the Orange Bowl stadium and kill thousands of people.

An embarrassment of big-name credits drove the film's popularity. Its director, first, was John Frankenheimer already famous for *The Manchurian Candidate* (1962), and its music score was written by John William's who was fresh off the successes of *Jaws* (1975) and *Star Wars* (1977). The Goodyear Corporation lent its blimp (and pilot) to the filmmakers and the National Football League allowed scenes for the film to be shot in the Orange Bowl stadium during Super Bowl X between the Dallas Cowboys and the Pittsburgh Steelers. Film footage from the game itself was incorporated into the movie.

The movie's terrorist plot exploited public anxieties hanging over from the 1972 attack by the Palestinian Black September group on the Israeli athletes assembled in Munich, Germany for the Olympic games. And what could excite the mixture of stealth and horror germane to the emergent notion of PTSD better than movie posters with the nose of an outsized blimp silently creeping over the lip of a stadium as masses of fans erupt in panic?

What theater goers knew but the terrified football fans portrayed in the film did not, was that the blimp's pilot was acting-out the anger he brought home from Vietnam about the public's failure to support the war effort. Michael Lander the pilot, played by Bruce Dern, was a one-man Freikorps avenging the war that had been lost to home-front flaccidity. The screenplay for Lander was loaded with sexual innuendo referring to America's degraded masculinity and its sublimation of military values by spectator sports—the same theme drummed by Italian and German fascists a half-century earlier.

Black Sunday was also the first film to nail together symptoms of dysfunction brought from the war with their representation as medical/psychiatric phenomenon. Whereas films like *Blood of Ghastly Horror* hinted at the connection with an admixture of war wounds and sci-fi technology, Dern's Lander actually presents his symptoms to a psychiatrist—and us, thereby involving our collaboration in the medicalizing of his experience that might otherwise have been understood to be political.

Coming Home. The influence of *Black Sunday* on the health care professionals who constructed PTSD may be only inferential, confirmation of that legacy conceivably laying in the archives left by its principal authors. But betrayed vets were soon a Hollywood staple and *Coming Home* (1978) was a more obvious contribution to that trend. The casting of Bruce Dern, once again, in the role of a wigged-out and sexually dysfunctional vet, was itself a framing device signaling movie goers that *Coming Home* was should be viewed as sequelae to *Black Sunday*. In it, Dern plays Bob the veteran who comes home to Sally, played by Jane Fonda. Sally is having an affair with another veteran, Luke, played by Jon Voigt, and she has become an opponent of the war. Luke is a paraplegic and sexually impotent. Luke, too, opposes the war and, consistent with the psychologizing of political behavior provided by the champions of PVS (the emerging notion of PTSD), *Coming Home* portrays Luke's politics as a form of catharsis. *Coming Home* ends with Bob going into a rage. After threatening to kill Sally and Luke, he commits suicide.

Coming Home added to the list of a dozen films portraying Vietnam veterans as deranged, armed, and dangerous. It also gendered the betrayal of the military more graphically than any film prior to it. The Fonda character, Sally, was direct in that regard: she was unfaithful to her soldier-husband and turned against the war while he was in combat. More interesting was the way filmmakers used images of masculinity to build the betrayal narrative. Bob's sexuality is problematized for us throughout the film. The bedroom scenes leave us wondering if his sexual performance meets his own standard of male machismo. His return from Vietnam to an adulteress wife is enough to destroy even a healthy sense of sexual self—but Waldo Salt, the screenwriter who won an Academy Award for the script, gives us still more. Sally's impotent lover, Luke, is apparently able to give her more satisfaction than the virile Bob! Bob discovers that, not only can't he give her what he wants, but that she doesn't need what he wants to give her. She has in effect rejected the conventional appeal of masculinity in favor of a man who, by the usual standard, is less than a man. Bob is betrayed, in other words, by more than just a member of the opposite sex: it is not only "the feminine" that *Coming Home* equates with deception and betrayal, but flaccidity in all forms.

In its production, *Coming Home* also networked powerful figures in the Hollywood film establishment and the Los Angeles medical community for the art–science synergy necessary to configure something as powerful as the cultural narrative formed by PTSD would be. *Coming Home* was the brainchild of Jane Fonda, and she writes in her 2005 autobiography that Ron Kovic had inspired the story. Through Kovic, Fonda was led to Shad Meshad at the Brentwood VA hospital and the psychiatrist Leonard Neff who teamed with writers Bruce Gilbert and Nancy Dowd to begin work on a film about Vietnam veterans with post-war issues. One of Gilbert's drafts featured a vet who armed himself and took to the wooded hills around Los Angeles in pursuit of his freedom from authorities—the storyline leading to the Rambo series that would blend the creative juices of artists and sciences still more densely.

Rambo. *Rambo* qua spectacle in the backstory of PTSD's rise in psychiatric practice and public awareness is hard to overstate. Like the spectacles of early modernism designed to "sell" science to the public, the character John Rambo, a Vietnam veteran played by Sylvester Stallone, and the elements of the *Rambo* story itself, stirred together images and themes drawn from both indigenous and contemporary ways of life and warfare while blurring the boundaries between what's "mad" and what's "bad"—the medical/psychiatric and the criminal.

To begin with, Rambo, the on-screen character, is described for us as being from "Native American and German" decent. With "native American" being the archetypical primitive and nomadic other of a settled America, and "German" evocative of the restrained and orderly stereotype of modern rationality— reminding of the scientific expertise that Germany had harnessed for death camps and military might in World War II —the polarity in his identity could not have been more tightly drawn. Rambo's weapon of choice, a large knife, reveals his primal instinct to survive by his own wits, while his proficiency with automatic weapons and skill for piloting a helicopter credential him as "the right stuff" for the late twentieth century.[22]

Drifting alone through the rural Pacific Northwest, Rambo is arrested for vagrancy and confined in a small-town jail. In pursuit of his freedom, he turns not to the bourgeois institutions of courts and lawyers, but the skills innate to the free-range warrior that he is; he manually overpowers the jailers and escapes into the woods.

Rambo is the stand-in for an untamed masculinity at odds with the domestication characteristic of modern bourgeois life. The post-Vietnam War drifter films such as *Ruckus* (1980), *The Stunt Man* (1980), *The Pursuit of D.B. Cooper* (1981), and *First Blood* captured the reality that it was the veteran who often rejected the conventions of mainstream America—not the other way around, as would efforts to symptomatize veteran unsettledness as trauma-related eventually try to have it. For many veterans, life on the road, at the margins of society, on the edge, was preferable to the mindless humdrum of the middle. It was a Nietzschean theme illuminating the mundane and repressive side of American culture, a paradigm shift in which the normal became problematic. The spectacle of these new-age veterans brought to the screen invited a response by the cultural status quo, a call for the intervention of the mental health establishment.

The campaign for the recognition of diagnostic nomenclature covering war trauma was waged in psychology, psychiatry, and sociology organizations as well as the Veterans Administration and Congressional committees. A turning point in the effort came in 1975 with the formation of the Vietnam Veterans Working Group. The VVWG included Shatan, psychiatrist Leonard Neff who had worked at the Los Angeles Brentwood VA, and Robert Lifton famous for the notion of "survivor's guilt" developed in his study of Holocaust survivors. The group came together after the American Psychological Association convention in Anaheim, CA at which Shatan remembered Neff for having "*dramatized* the dynamics of combat-related stress" [emphasis added] with the following anecdote:

A vet escaped from the Brentwood VA and laid siege to some police cars. The vet was armed and took over a patrol car. Neff rushed to the scene and determined that [the vet] was having a flashback. So Neff called out to him, "Attention! This is Captain Neff. The mission is accomplished. You don't have to fight any more. Lay down your arms." The vet surrendered peacefully.[23]

With Shatan's editorial qualification of the story as a dramatization, its meaning lies as much in its interpretation as its details. It's hard to imagine film buffs *not* exclaiming, "Hey, those words are right out of the first *Rambo* film!" And they would be right: Rambo's former commander Colonel Trautman talks him down saying, "The mission is over, Rambo … It's over." On the other hand, news junkies familiar with the actual event on which the anecdote was based, as reported at the time by *The Los Angeles Times*, might know that the real-life vet had not "escaped" from anyplace, there was no stolen police car, no reference to "flashbacks," and no movie-ready lines such as those attributed to Neff in the anecdote.

However, the upstream provenance of the anecdote and its impact downstream both underscore the power of film *qua* spectacle to influence the thinking of mental health professionals. Shatan recounted the anecdote to sociologist Wilber Scott in 1988, well after the 1982 release of *First Blood*. There is no way of knowing how accurately Shatan remembered Neff's 1975 anecdote, but it seems more than likely that there was some Rambo bootlegged into his memory. Even more interesting as provenance is the likelihood that by the late 1980s, when sociologist Scott interviewed Shatan, that medical culture in Los Angeles was so saturated with Hollywood-made Vietnam veteran imagery that Shatan was no longer sensitive to the putative boundary between art and science, so that the similarity of Neff's words that he repeated to Scott to the lines from *First Blood* did not sound significant. In other words, the fact that the APA convention held seven years *before* the film was remembered a dozen years *after* the film through the lens *of* the film is testimony to the film's power as spectacle.

The impact of the 1975 APA convention on the incubation of new terminology for war trauma is recorded by Scott in his 1993 book *The Politics of Readjustment: Vietnam Veterans since the War*. The third edition of American Psychiatric Association's DSM came out in 1980 with the new category, PTSD included. A construct of well-meaning professionals, it was a label with potential to help thousands of veterans dealing with post-war issues. But as Paul Starr pointed out in *The Discarded Army: Veterans after Vietnam*, it also had the danger of imputing to veterans psychological characteristics that were not their own and publicly stigmatize them as victims. The projection of the victim-veteran image into popular and political culture would, in turn, displace the memory that thousands of veterans had been radicalized by their wartime experience and help rewrite the history of the war as something that happened *to* America.[24]

Victim-Veterans and Victim-Nations

The availability of the victim–veteran–nation narrative to journalists, pundits, and historians added a choice to how the memory of the war would be constructed. By the 1980s, the political climate of the country was changing and the marginalization of Vietnam veterans through the medicalization of their image was tailored for the times. From 1980 on, almost all Vietnam War movies were actually stories about the coming-home experiences of veterans and the difficulties they faced in their post-war lives—and nary one of them was portrayed as physically or psychologically healthy.

The prevalence of the wounded/damaged veteran in popular culture dovetailed with the political right's mantra that it was liberal "softness" that had sold-out the military mission in Vietnam and deprived the men who fought the pride of victory. And now, the argument ran, liberalism reproduced an infectious permissiveness that threatened to rot the nation from within.

PTSD also doubled as a credential, a way for veterans to claim the unseen, the "wound on the inside" as it came to be called, as a badge of honor, a kind of Purple Heart. A 1983 article in the *American Journal of Psychiatry* reported five cases whereupon men had presented PTSD symptoms. Three of the men said they were former prisoners of war. "In fact," the authors found, "none had been prisoners of war, four [of the five] had never been in Vietnam, and two had never even been in the military." The claims of psychiatric damage with no apparent material causes became so common that the term "factitious PTSD" was coined to categorize them.[25] Well into the twenty-first century, it remained nevertheless common for the press to report that 30–50% of Vietnam veterans suffered from PTSD—even though only about 15% of US soldiers there saw combat.

By the time troops embarked for the Persian Gulf in 1990, it was not uncommon to hear men of the Vietnam generation claiming a combat-veteran identity with the boast, "I'm 100% PTSD." Operation Desert Storm, as it was called, was hardly a war so it was no surprise that the return of troops was accompanied by conflicted emotions and imagery. With no war stories to tell and virtually no wounds for display, *virtual* wounds became the currency of authenticity. Sleeping disorders, lethargy, depression, mysterious rashes, unexplained cancers—none of it confirmed by epidemiological studies—quickly dominated the coming-home narrative. Coming home sick, it seemed, was the way to say, "I'm the real-deal combat veteran." The conflation of wounds, seen or unseen, with martial accomplishment was by then so ingrained in the culture that expectations mutually held by soldiers, their families and friends, was that "hurt" was the only honorable way to come home.

Troops headed to Iraq in the spring of 2003 with their homecoming already scripted: they would return with PTSD—news reporters said so. And reporters were all too ready to fulfill their own prophecy. By July, only four months after the deployments, the first of the invasion forces began returning home and the *Christian Science Monitor* couldn't wait: "The Other Battle, Coming Home," it headlined before reminding readers that 50% of Vietnam veterans suffer PTSD. Within weeks the media had settled into storylines that displaced controversies over what the war was about with comparisons with the war in Vietnam, many using data about Vietnam veterans to make points about troops returning from the Middle East. In their 2009 media study, psychologists Thomas Armstrong and Bunmi Olatunji reported an "explosion of coverage of PTSD in soldiers" after 2003 that rocketed to 211% increase between 2006 and 2008. By then, virtually every news organization in the country had done a feature story or special report on troubled veterans.[26]

One of the largest and most powerful entries on the list was *Boston Globe*'s four-part series "The War after the War" that began on October 29, 2006. It featured veterans prone to violence with substance abuse problems and difficulties in maintaining home and work lives after service in Iraq. Its 20,000 words accompanied by an online photo gallery left little room for thinking outside the PTSD block. The *New York Times* followed with a series that began in January 2008 with a 5,600-word feature story set off by montage of twenty-four miniaturized photographs of men's faces on the front page of a Sunday edition. Under the headline "Across America, Deadly Echoes of Foreign Battles," reporters Deborah Sontag and Lizette Alvarez told about the large numbers of Iraq and Afghanistan War veterans charged with homicide; about a third of their victims being spouses, girlfriends, and children—the point of the series being that the legal defense of the accused veterans could be strengthened with a diagnosis of PTSD used to construct an alibi for their violence.[27]

The morphing of PTSD, a medical category, into a symbol with legal implications highlighted its susceptibility for use as a trope, a symbol with meaning separate from that to which it originally referred. The discourse of trauma has displaced almost all else from the coming-home news coverage of our current generation of veterans. In their 2013 book *Beyond PTSD*, the anthropologists Sarah Hautzinger and Jean Scandlyn write, "In most conversations where the topic of returning soldiers [comes up], PTSD is mentioned in the first few minutes."[28]

The twin images of soldiers bringing the war home with them as "hidden injuries" of trauma, and soldiers disparaged by liberals and radicals as villains in an unpopular war were vivified in American imagination following the US defeat in Vietnam.[29] The task of debunking those images is assisted by what we now know about shellshock and, in the case of veterans defiled on the home front, the mythical character of the German stab-in-the-back legend.[30]

The "unseen wound" of trauma gained legitimacy with the inclusion of PTSD in the 1980 DSM, but the same sort of empirical issues that challenged the veracity of shellshock—recall those shellshock patients never exposed to exploding shells—dogged the validity of PTSD.

It seems clear that the prevalence of trauma imagery in the media portrayals of US soldiers returning from Vietnam and recent wars in the Middle East works as a spectacle the same way, as did the stab-in-back-legend in Germany: to form a betrayal narrative for defeat. Brought to life for Americans after Vietnam in Hollywood films like *Black Sunday, Coming Home*, and the *Rambo* series, the real war seemed to have been at home. And, as Rambo had it, it was on the home front that the war was lost, a loss to be avenged through attacks on individuals and groups deemed to have sapped our manliness: liberals in Congress, radicals on campus, and a seditious femininity that erodes our will-to-war.[31] Lost in the fog of victim-veteran constructions is the real story that thousands of active-duty personnel and veterans turned against the war, the same interplay of remembering and forgetting that erased the public memory that thousands of German soldiers had rebelled against their military leaders by the end of the war.

With its defeat in Vietnam, the United States lost confidence in its place as "City on the Hill," becoming a nation of hurt, not hope; an avenging victim-nation with frightening resemblance to Germany and Italy following World War I; and having suffered the shock and trauma of defeat, it now inflicts "shock and awe" on others. Like inter-war Germany, Americans are soaking in a revanchist political culture that longs for a restoration of a mythical America, an America that never was.

The cycle of lost wars begetting more wars has extended into the twenty-first century. The so-called Vietnam syndrome that President George H.W. Bush said the United States "kicked" with its Persian Gulf venture in 1991 remains, nevertheless, the motor-force driving the nation's need to restore the global dominance and status it feels was lost in Vietnam. That cycle has come with a new generation of war-trauma symptoms and diagnostic terminology of which traumatic brain injury (TBI) is the most well known. And like with shellshock and PTSD, TBI was brought to prominence by a spectacle having little to do with scientific practice.

Before getting to the case history of TBI, though, Chapter 4 delves into the mental health implications of Agent Orange poisoning, a story in which we see the role of news and movies as non-science factors in the science of war trauma played in spectacular fashion.

Notes

1   Scott, *The Politics of Readjustment*, 60. As reportedly told by Leonard Neff to the 1975 convention of the American Psychological Association and relayed years later to sociologist Wilber Scott by psychiatrist Chaim Shatan.

2   Lines spoken by the character Trautman in the film *First Blood* (1982) the first of the Rambo film series.

3   Wells, *The War Within*.

4   The phrase was a popular idiom in Vietnam expressing opposition to military authority. Film maker David Zeiger made it the title of his 2006 film documenting the resistance to the war within the military itself.

5   After the notoriety given him by *Ramparts*, Duncan became a popular figure in the opposition the war. See the *New York Times* obituary for Duncan at Donald W. Duncan, 79, Ex-Green Beret and Early Critic of Vietnam War, Is Dead, *New York Times*, May 6, 2016.

6   News Release, 1966.

7   Bojarski's letter was reproduced as a leaflet titled "GIs in Vietnam want to come Home!" Fifth Avenue Peace Parade Committee files, Wisconsin State Historical Society Library.

8   Coyne, *The Impudent Snobs*.

9 Cook, "The Real Conspiracy Exposed."

10 Conrad and Schneider, *Deviance and Medicalization.*

11 Bourne, *Men, Stress, and Vietnam*, 73.

12 Clements, *Witness to War.*

13 Bourne, *Men, Stress, and Vietnam*, 21, 40–43, 76, 96. The adrenal secretion referred to (p. 21) is 17-hydroxycorticosteroid.

14 It is a troubling thought that, had the medical professionals who waged the war they did for the legitimation of what became PTSD known the history of their own field, i.e., the shaky standing of shellshock as a diagnostic category, they would probably have spent their time and effort elsewise.

15 According to Bourne, *Men Stress and Vietnam*, 40, "… antiwar sentiment in the United States appears to have had little effect upon the motivational level of the troops in the field." He adds that "the morale of American troops in Vietnam has remained as high or higher than any previous war."

16 Scott, *The Politics of Readjustment*, 38.

17 Ibid., 38.

18 Nordheimer, "From Dak To to Detroit."

19 Ibid.

20 Romo quoted by Kifner, "Veterans Face Guardsmen."

21 *The Lively Set* (1964) and *Bus Riley" Back in Town* (1965) are examples.

22 Rambo's ethnicity is defined for us in In *Rambo First Blood: Part II*, the second film in the series.

23 Scott, *The Politics of Readjustment.* 60.

24 Starr, *The Discarded Army*; Starr, "Home from the War."

25 For "factitious PTSD" see Sparr and Pankratz, "Factitious Posttraumatic Stress Disorder" and Lynn and Belza, "Factitious Posttraumatic Stress Disorder." Hagopian, *The Vietnam in American Memory*, 73 writes that Jack McCloskey, team leader of the San Francisco Waller Street vet center, funded by the Veterans Administration outreach program, refused to check the DD-214 discharge papers of new clients before counseling them. As a result, says Hagopian, "some of the clients his staff saw turned out not to have been Vietnam veterans at all."

26 Armstrong and Olatunji, "PTSD in the Media," 57. The *Pittsburgh Tribune-Review* (February 2004), the *Washington Post* (November 2004) and *USA Today* (October 2007) were among the major trend setters.

27 With a reference to the Sontag and Alvarez report, I wrote here about the *Times'* seeming fixation with PTSD: www.counterpunch.org/2014/04/17/war-trauma-and-the-new-york-times/

28 Hautzinger and Scandlyn, *Beyond Post-Traumatic Stress,* 16.

29 I wrote about the myth of spat-upon veterans in *The Spitting Image.*

30 Theweleit, *Male Fantasies.*

31 The actress Jane Fonda was scapegoated for the loss of the war (see Lembcke *Hanoi Jane,* 163). Historian Elaine May in *Fortress America* describes conservative fears that post-WWII urbanization had shifted parental influence over boys from fathers to mothers, resulting in a generation of young men ill-suited for the military—a supposed consequence known as "momism."

4
AGENT ORANGE

As Spectacle and Trope

TBI could be the next Agent Orange.

(Paul Rieckhoff, *Big Think*)[1]

TBI, like agent orange (AO)? What in the world is media critic and political science professor Paul Rieckhoff talking about? AO is a chemical compound, a weed spray; TBI is a mental and emotional condition, a diagnostic category. Fibromyalgia the next iPhone? It makes about as much sense.

Trying to make sense of a puzzling health condition through analogy with a new technology, be it the defoliant AO or an IT device, makes nonsense of sensemaking. It's an endeavor like, well, that proverbial research error of comparing apples to oranges.

But what if enough people understood "apple" to mean "orange"? What if the association of words with objects like fruit was shown to be arbitrary, a figment of indeterminant origin but prolonged use? Jean Baudrillard, the French theorist of post-modernism, tells us that words are signs with an attenuated and artificial connection to what they reference. Gendered pronouns, for example, are *just* words that have social connotations separate from the body parts they supposedly refer to. In like fashion, we'll see here that the words "agent orange" are *just* words, signifying a dangerous chemical in one context while transfiguring into a medical category in another context.

"Seeing" and Remembering the War

The most impactful and enduring memories of the war in Vietnam are forged by visual imagery that combine elements of human trauma and modern technology.

DOI: 10.4324/9781003391906-5

The young girl Kim Phuc running naked toward Nick Ut's camera with burns suffered from the napalm attack on her village of Trang Bang in 1972 is one of the most captivating of the sort.

Some of the iconic images testify as much to the spectacle-making power of modern photography and film: Eddie Adams's 1968 photo of General Nguyen Ngoc Loan executing a Vietcong prisoner on a Saigon street with a shot to head in which we see the bullet blowing out the side of Nguyen Van Lem's head that would not have been captured by the lower lens speed of earlier cameras; the camera shots of Huey helicopters settling in landing zones with the whump, whump, whump of their rotary blades edited-in to conjure for viewers the sensual experience of the combat awaiting the troops jumping from the choppers. These were the obligatory scenes for Hollywood renditions of the war for decades to come.[2] And like the fascination with a cat in the tree being as much with the crowd watching the cat as with the cat itself, described by Tobias Myers in Chapter 1, the fascination of post-Vietnam War audiences with the sights and sounds of war was as much with themselves as viewers and listeners—themselves as subject—as with the content of what was seen and heard.

The Vietnam War imagery made popular in newscasts and film blended aesthetic appeal, political function, and technological awe the way Falasca-Zamponi thought characteristic of the fascist culture of the 1930s. And few things in America's Vietnam War experience were more diversely attractive to media and public attention than AO: a chemical weapon that decimated triple-canopy jungle and was the presumptive root of many post-war physical ailments that grew to encompass veterans' postwar trauma.

Imaging Agent Orange

Just as many people are surprised to learn that PTSD did not exist as a mental health term until 1980, and that it was brought into being by the attention drawn to Vietnam veterans' opposition to the war, so will readers of David Zierler's 2011 book *The Invention of Ecocide* be surprised that it was that same veterans' movement that made AO an environmental and health issue. Without that movement, he writes, "there is little reason to believe that the herbicide scientists would have advanced their agenda had they embarked on a public relations mission to gather popular support."[3] In less tangled prose, Zierler is suggesting that it was influences external to scientists and their work that encouraged the application of scientific method to the issues presented by the legacy of AO use in Vietnam.

The surge of attention given AO in the late 1970s and early 1980s was a multimedia phenomenon involving television news, Hollywood film, and photography that brought veterans back to center stage for a reprise of their role as damaged and forgotten victims of the war. The nodal historical events for that convergence were Chicago CBS affiliate WBBM's broadcast on March 23, 1978, of the news special *Agent Orange: Vietnam's Deadly Fog*, and its remake for the 1986 film *Unnatural Causes: The Agent Orange Story* that transformed its documentarian qualities into entertainment spectacle. In the backstory to those events, we see the interplay of political, scientific, and informational forces that pushed AO onto the stage.

The Quiet Backstory to Agent Orange

Early critical perspectives on AO, were driven by the "war crimes movement," according to Zierler, for which the scientific concern was with the strategic prowess and legal standing of herbicides within the international rules of war, not public health, veteran war trauma, or even ecology. The British had been the first to use an AO precursor in their Malay colony to kill the dense jungle foliage that communist insurgents were thought to use as cover for military activity. In that sense, claimed the British, the herbicide use was not an antipersonnel weapon— i.e. not a danger to people—and therefore not illegal. The United States adopted the same reasoning when it introduced AO to Vietnam as Operation Ranch Hand in early 1962.

To the extent that the American people were at all aware of AO use, it was not thought to be injurious to human health but something rather benign—like a weed killer.[4] The first *New York Times* story to even mention AO came on September 20, 1966, over four years after its use in Vietnam began. The story distinguished between defoliants like AO and *antipersonnel* weapons by separately mentioning CS (Corson-Stoughton Gas), a form of tear gas, as an example of the latter. Defoliants, said by Pentagon officials to be sprayed by aircraft, were cast in a defensive role:

> to strip trees of all foliage along a path about 85 feet in width that helps expose enemy roads and supply trains ... increasing the effectiveness of air strikes and help[ing] foil possible enemy ambushes.

In October 1962, agent blue had begun to be used to kill agricultural crops in order to deprive guerrilla units of food. Even those actions would be presented in American news coverage as attacks against plant life, not human life, implying that their purpose was defensive. It would be years before Americans, including veterans, would understand that the poisoning of large agricultural areas forced peasants off their land and into Strategic Hamlets.[5]

"Earth Day Was a Snow Job"—I.F. Stone

In 1957 Columbia University's dean Louis Hacker reviewed Ludwig Von Mises's new book *Theory and History*. Von Mises, he said, named "environmentalism" as one of several "anti-capitalist" social forces playing havoc in modern economic theory.[6] At the time, the book and Hacker's review in the *New York*

Times were important on their own terms and in retrospect their recognition of environmentalism might seem unremarkable. Rachael Carson, troubled then by humankind's disrespect for nature, would soon write *Silent Spring* that would launch a movement that would climax on the first Earth Day in 1970. Or so goes the received history of the environmental movement.

Earth Day's arrival on the historical stage is actually more complicated, snarling accounts of its history in a chicken-and-egg conundrum. Did a few well-placed visionaries like the Washington University biologist Barry Commoner and Senator Gaylord Nelson found a movement when they conceived Earth Day?[7] Or did the movement make the Day, as is popularly believed decades later, with Rachael Carson revered as its creator? If neither of these, what then?

The movement-made-the-day narrative has currency because organizations like the Sierra Club, formed in 1892, and the Audubon Society, formed in 1905, had for years been advocating the protection of nature; the Wilderness Act had been passed in 1964 and the Clean Air Act in 1970.[8] With all the ingredients on hand for an Earth Day before April of 1970, why then and not before?

What was missing was the holism implicit in the *ism* of environmentalism, the suffix connoting a value system, a belief in and commitment to priorities and principles that were both free-standing and inter-related: conservation and preservation with sustainable use, nature-centered and humanist, rational and scientific but faith-based as well.

In fact, environmentalism per se had little presence in American consciousness before the first Earth Day. The "environmentalism" in Louis Hacker's review of the Von Mises book was the *only* time between 1955 and 1960 that the word can be found in the *Times*. And from there, its prominence plummeted—to zero entries in the *Times* from 1960 to 1965, before having a comeback to 1 between 1965 and the eve of Earth Day in 1970. While all the ingredients for environmentalism were on hand before 1970, the social chemistry needed for them to be a movement was missing. And the war in Vietnam was the stick that stirred the pot.[9]

Even then, Earth Day's initial public identity was as much about what it was *not*—the war in Vietnam—as what it *was* about. The first major news coverage of the then-forthcoming Earth Day was a March 9 *New York Times* story headlined as "Student Activists Turning from Campus to Society." The story made a passing reference to the 1969 Moratorium Day demonstrations against the war that had closed schools, churches, and businesses for a day of reflection just five months earlier on October 15 (Chapter 3). But with stunning blindness to the imminent invasion of Cambodia on April 30, the killing of four students at Kent State University who protested the invasion, and the subsequent eruption of student strikes that would soon shutdown many of the country's campuses, the *Times* story went on to past-tense the war as if it was over: students "were groping … to find an issue with the galvanizing appeal once provided by the Vietnam War," according to the reporter. The day after Earth Day, April 23, the *Times's* Jack

Gould surveyed the television news coverage of the day's events and made no mention of any attention given Vietnam, defoliation, AO, or veterans.

On May 11, in the midst of the largest student uprising in US history following the invasion of Cambodia and the students shot dead at Kent State on May 4, the *Times* headlined a story with "No Mass Rallies Seen Likely" about a small antiwar rally on the Capital Mall in Washington, D.C. the day before; the story cited complaints that the protesters had left behind clutter and garbage—unlike the Earth Day kids who had cleaned-up nicely a couple weeks earlier.

But Earth Day was *clearly* about Vietnam. According to the celebrated muckraking journalist at the time, I.F. Stone, Earth Day was "a gigantic snow job." "In his eyes," wrote historian Leslie Paul Thiele,

> it was a diversion: "Just as the Caesars once used bread and circuses," Stone wrote, "so ours use rock and roll, idealism, and noninflammatory social issues to turn the youth off from more urgent concerns which might really threaten our power structure." Stone was thinking of the war in Indochina … Stone may have had a point.[10]

And if Stone had a point, Vietnam veterans were its sharp edge. Like the formulation of PTSD as a diagnostic category that took shape as a foil against their activism, so too did environmentalism function as an antidote to even more threatening developments in the political culture—antiwar Vietnam veterans among them.

There was a latent environmentalism in Stone's antiwar position which, tragically, would not be recognized for decades. A 2022 Webinar on the climate crisis facing the nation and world pointed to US militarism as a major contributor to environmental warming and depletion of energy resources: "The US military is the world's single largest institutional consumer of fossil fuels … and the single largest institutional emitter of greenhouse gases," read the invitation to the Webinar. The forum neglected to mention the military as a gunslinger for Big Oil, propping up petrol-friendly governments in the Middle East and overthrowing those like Libya's that dared to nationalize its oil fields. One can only imagine where we would be environmentally if the power of the anti-militarism amassed in the 1960s and 1970s had not been eclipsed by the environmental movement and, instead, sustained its focus on militarism. Might I.F. Stone's bumper sticker for that counterfactual history be written, "No Big Guns, No Big Oil, No Climate Crisis"?[11]

"Kissing the earth goodbye" is the way Michael Klare punctuated I.F. Stone's point. As fighting between Russia and US-backed Ukraine raged in 2022, Klare, Professor of Peace and World Security Studies at Hampshire College, warned that the war's greatest casualty

> could be planet earth itself. He cited the toll of wounded and killed in the war, the number of displaced civilians, and the destruction of infrastructure and

went on to describe even greater collateral damage: agricultural land ruined in Ukraine, funds to mediate climate-warming diverted to military priorities, and the virtual elimination of superpower diplomacy to address climate change. All this, Klare says, points to elites pursuing geo-political military strategies ahead of planet survival.[12]

Veterans and Agent Orange

The October 15, 1969, Moratorium Day had been a coming-out event for VVAW, the organized expression of veterans' opposition to the war. Its network of underground newspapers and off-base coffee houses had educated replacement troops headed for Vietnam about the futility and immorality of the war; subsequently, the Moratorium spirit spread quickly among GIs in Vietnam. Ground troops supportive of the Moratorium wore black armbands on October 15; some even refused orders to go on patrol; there was a spike in attacks by enlisted men on their own officers, called "fragging." The situation was "more than enough to worry the Pentagon," according to historian Marilyn Young. And it was getting worse. In the summer of 1971 Marine Colonel Robert Heinl would write, "our army that now remains in Vietnam is in a state approaching collapse, with individual units avoiding or having refused combat, murdering their officers … and dispirited where not near mutinous "[13]

The veterans' threat to blow the lid off atrocities committed by US forces in Vietnam, covered up by authorities, raised the greatest alarms. The first reports of a massacre at My Lai in March of 1968 appeared in *The New York Times* just after the October 1969 Moratorium. "New members flocked to VVAW" after those reports, according to historian Andrew Hunt. Weeks later, a group called Citizens' Commission of Inquiry on U.S. War Crimes in Vietnam formed and announced plans to hold hearings in which veterans and service personnel could testify. The first was scheduled for Annapolis, MD, just days before Earth Day.[14]

Amidst this, the absence of the Vietnam veteran voice in Earth Day was itself a kind of elephant in the room, an absence that with its own presence validated Stone's comment that the environmental discourse channeled the attention and energies of reform-minded campus activists into safer waters: as he put it elsewhere, "Who could be against the environment?"

The discursive disconnect between the environmental movement launched by Earth Day, on the one hand, and the environmental implications inherent in the herbicidal bombing of Vietnam, on the other, was conspicuous. Going forward, the veterans enshrouded in that warp would fall prey to further ploys using medical framings to reshape their experience, displacing altogether antiwar veterans from public memory of the war and postwar years.[15]

In retrospect, we can see the outlines of a post-war culture that would mature in the 1980s into a pernicious betrayal narrative for the lost war. The images of trauma-stricken veterans being drawn by pundits and professions committed to the PTSD discourse were the most pronounced figures in that outline; suggestions of veterans traumatized by exposure to AO would give it even shaper definition.

Injuries attributed to AO came with a materiality—physical damage to the body—the paucity of which had bedeviled war trauma diagnoses going back to shellshock of the WWI era. In that sense, its addition to the trauma analytics was a *now-found* missing link. Its physicality could be documented with the camera. Its visual imagery—pictures of children with hideously deformed faces and missing and twisted arms and legs—could move professional and public imaginations in ways that other claims to PTSD's authenticity could not. The photographs of AO's human damage were definitional spectacles!

There was, finally, the *silent*-killer character to AO, the submarine-like weapon that lay hidden in the victim's organs and tissues only to explode years later. And with that came the anxiety about who did and did not come home with the killer in them and when it would strike and the paranoia about *who* had put the stalker in play and take responsibility for the damage it was wreaking.

The first concerns about AO effects on humans were voiced in Vietnamese newspapers in June of 1969. Independent surveys of South Vietnamese hospitals and interviews with refugees conducted in Hanoi followed and a committee appointed by the National Academy of Science (NAS) in the United States reported that "it could find no conclusive relationship between exposure to herbicides and birth defect in humans." In his letter of transmittal for the report, the president of NAS said, "On balance, the untoward effects of the herbicide program on the health of the Vietnamese people appear to have been smaller than one might have feared."[16]

In a 1981 study for the Air Command and Staff College, Air Force major Alvin L. Young emphasized that it was "*extremely difficult* to find precise information concerning the adverse effects" of herbicides including those containing dioxin (TCDD), the highly toxic "nasty and curious compound that made agent orange notorious (emphasis in the original)."[17] Young reviewed findings from dozens of industrial case studies of TCDD exposure and concluded that "there are no epidemiologic data associating TCDD with any long-term health effects in humans other than chloracne." While acknowledging "neither is there strong evidence to validate the absence of such effects ... there is currently no reliable evidence that links dioxin exposure to cancer or birth defect in humans."[18]

If it's true, as often said, that perception is nine-tenths of reality, then there were enough details in AO's effectiveness as an herbicidal weapon for critics to imagine its effects, as well, on enemy troops and populations. Afterall, a weapon used to deprive civilians of food and shelter, as AO was for the Strategic Hamlet program, can be easily perceived as an antipersonnel weapon, with health effects on civilian noncombatants.

Activist's fears about the long-term environmental and human damage of AO's use in Vietnam reached into the twenty-first century. In his 2011 book *Scorched Earth: Legacies of Chemical warfare in Vietnam*, Fred Wilcox wrote that by 1965 45% of the spraying was directed at crops. His descriptions of children with horrendous birth defects are accompanied with gut-wrenching photographs taken on his visit to a children's care center; interviews with the children's parents associate the damaged bodies with AO poisoning of crop land.[19]

Association is not causation, of course, and debates go on about the strength of claims about AO and birth defects in Vietnam. But it was the *perception* that an herbicide that killed food crops would be toxic to humans that drifted into the American victim-veteran narrative that was forming in the 1990s; and it was the spectacle of birth defects that vaulted AO into the mental health debate.

A lack of evidence nevertheless continued to vex the claims that US veterans had been hurt by AO. In 2011, David Zierler wrote that, "Epidemiological studies on U.S. veterans dating back twenty years have so far been unable to establish a conclusive link between AO and a variety of cancers and other health maladies that some servicemen have attributed to the herbicide."[20] For his 2012 book *Agent Orange*, historian Edwin Martini reviewed the disagreements between the White House Agent Orange Working Group assembled by the Carter administration in 1979, which had been unable to say anything conclusive about the human effects of AO, and the Center for Disease Control (CDC), which used different methods to assess those effects. The CDC's eclectic approach led to squabbles over how to measure troop exposures to dioxin levels the consequences of exposures.[21] Retired Major General John Murray had adjudicated tensions between those studies and Martini quoted his conclusions:

> In view of the limitation of records, restriction of the criteria, the unlimited expression of doubts, and the scientific inability because of these doubts to arrive at conclusions the continuance of this Agent Orange study is an exercise in futility.

Judging Murray's conclusion to be "consistent and clear,"[22] Martini surmised that "science could simply not answer the types of questions being asked about the effects of human exposure to AO and that their answers awaited political decisions."[23] He was right, except that science and politics both awaited the interventions of news media and popular culture.

1978: Agent Orange Comes Out

AO lay dormant in news and popular culture throughout the 1970s. And when it did enter the American conversation, it was less for its scientific significance than as a set of *events* that combined news media, a movie, and folk-culture happenings.[24]

The game changer was the television news documentary that aired on the Chicago CBS affiliate WBBM-2 on March 23, 1978. Entitled *Agent Orange: Vietnam's Deadly Fog* and produced by news anchor Bill Kurtis, the program was prompted by a Chicago VA counselor, Maude De Victor. One of De Victor's clients, Charles Evens, was dying of cancer that he thought might have been caused by AO poisoning. It was the first time that De Victor had heard about the herbicide and her efforts to learn more were met with disinterest by higher levels of authority in the Veterans Administration (VA). Thinking that public pressure might move the bureaucracy, she sought publicity for what she was doing but drilled dry wells there as well. Then she caught the attention of WBBM's Kurtis.

Kurtis's receptivity to De Victor's approach echoes the *New York Times* agreement to publish psychiatrist Chaim Shatan's op-ed on war trauma in 1972 after previously rejecting it. As described in Chapter 3, it was the spectacle of antiwar Vietnam veterans in the street at the Republican Party national convention in Miami Beach that changed minds at the *Times*. Likewise, the appearance in theaters of *Taxi Driver* in 1976 and *Black Sunday* in 1977, two of the all-time most explicitly "crazy vet" films, just months before Kurtis committed to airing De Victor's findings, may have piqued his interest. In any case, the damaged veterans spotlighted in his report provided grist for the full-fledged psychologizing of AO that would follow.

Weak on facts—beginning with its acknowledgment that the NAS research had not found links between dioxin and effects on humans—the show compiled visuals that, nevertheless, led viewers to the exactly opposite conclusion: a generation of deformed babies awaited Vietnam veterans. Kurtis's strategy was an appeal to the power of emotion over the power of mind, the same technique of persuasion used in sixteenth-century salons to "sell" the superiority of science over religion that was described in Chapter 1. Kurtis's appropriation of techniques used by nineteenth-century charlatans selling snake-oil elixirs, and by twentieth-century Christian fundamentalist displaying jars of fetuses to excite public emotions about abortion, was obvious.[25] He juxtaposed a disembodied hand, said to be Vietnamese, with the deformed hand of an American veteran's son, and later admitted: "The picture [of the boy's fingertips] needed no narration. In an instant it communicated a message with an emotion that couldn't be forgotten. That is television's strength."[26]

Major Alvin Young's response to the WBBM broadcast was less about the program's dearth of scientific precision than its having exposed the properties inherent in the AO issue that lent it to the social construction of a new category of war trauma.

Young called the broadcast the "initial publicity" given the issue of health effects of herbicide use in Vietnam and observed that much of that publicity was "based on emotionally charged personal tragedies (e.g., the presence of terminal cancer in a young veteran)." With no scientific link between Dioxin and human health, Young speculated that "some other factor associated with the Vietnam war may be responsible, or, perhaps, the symptoms are afflictions of aging and attendant psycho-social aberrations."[27] The implications of Young's conjecture were made explicit by Martini:

> [Young's study] was the first major piece to adopt the idea that diseases believed to be related to agent orange exposure might actually be in some way social diseases, constructed in part around the intersecting matrices of memory, media, trauma and legitimate disease concerns ... Young proposed that agent orange had become a way for some veterans to make sense of their experiences, their trauma, and perhaps their other medical conditions.[28]

By 1980, AO was becoming a spectacle. Oddly, though, it was not the images of Vietnam stripped of its triple-canopy jungle that shocked Americans. Given the defoliated wastelands that would later become fixtures in American memories of the war, there were surprising few photographs in the 1970s of AO's impact on plant life. In the handful of *New York Times* stories on AO as of May 1973, none were accompanied by photographs. In fact, the first widely viewed imaging of AO may have been *Unnatural Causes*, the 1986 adaption for Hollywood of WBBM's documentary—with AO's damage portrayed as traumatized US war veterans, not Vietnamese forests.[29]

Agent Orange Goes to the Movies

EXT   LANDING ZONE   DAY   VIETNAM

A wave of Huey helicopters settling onto a landing zone. Troops pile out of the choppers and charge into a jungle firefight. A monster-looking fixed-wing aircraft lumbers overhead. Flying low and slow, its spray soaks the ground troops below. Dripping wet, they emerge from the tree line onto a desolate terrain. Chemical defoliation.

INT   VA OFFICE   CHICAGO

A VA benefits counselor bids a departing client good luck. Into her office steps a threatening figure who introduces himself: "I'm a walking time bomb," before adding, "I got the word on the VA, they cut you up for their experiment ... I got the word, from the 'lost ones.'" He taunts the counselor: "You think I'm crazy, don't you?" before she talks him down.

Mise en scenes from the war in Vietnam and its aftermath: the wumph, wumph, wumph of the chopper blades; GIs caught in a chemical dump; a veteran deranged by the war. The stage is set for a film mixing agent orange and PTSD—with no politicized veterans in the script.

Unnatural Causes in 1978 was a spectacle-making exercise that completed the transmogrification of AO's identity from an herbicide with military significance, to a toxic chemical compound allegedly dangerous to human biology, to a phrase endowed with psychological connotations. In its mental health iteration, the words "agent orange" became a simulacrum in which the chemical agent's causative identity got conflated with the condition it caused—the AO that made veterans sick would thenceforth also name the malady that it caused. When psychiatrist Charles Hoge compiled his list of synonyms for veterans' "postwar reactions," he included "Agent Orange syndrome" along with shellshock and the World War II label Battle Fatigue. It was that contorted meaning of AO that enabled Vietnam veteran and AO activist Berry Romo to remember, years later, that "people *with* agent orange" attended the first events opposing herbicidal warfare—that is, AO as a mental illness, not a vial of chemicals (emphasis added).[30]

Unnatural Causes was written by John Sayles, then fresh off his successes with *The Return of the Secaucus 7* and *Brother from Another Planet*. John Ritter as the film's veteran Frank Coleman was already a mega-star with Emmy and Golden Globe awards in *Three's Company*; Alfre Woodward cast as Maude De Victor had an Emmy for *Hill Street Blues* and an Academy Award nomination for *Cross Creek*. With those marquees, *Unnatural Causes* was destined for high ratings and critical praise—and a large audience for its conflations of chemical poisoning and war trauma.[31]

The "timebomb" veteran is given no name and does not appear in the film again making his cameo a preamble for the linkage between AO and mental health narrative that Sayles, the screenwriter, was constructing. With the chemical spraying depicted in the film's opening just minutes earlier, the figure of a hair-triggered human bomb becomes a framing device to cue viewers that the story to follow is only ostensibly about the *physio*logical damage left by spraying. The real damage is on the inside, the hidden injuries carried home from Vietnam in the minds and emotions of its veterans. The comments bespeaking wounded psyches permeate the hospital wards:

"Fuzzy … his elevator doesn't go to the top floor … at least when he came back."
"My old lady says I come back different."
"… he thinks he's got some baby-burning, acid-head Vietnam vet who's just going to snap someday …"
"… that's crazy Eddy there, he came in with a migraine and they give him a psych workup."
"Not a day goes by I don't think about Nam"
"These boys came back with their eggs scrambled."

Agent Orange: A Conversion Disorder

Unnatural Causes does not lose touch with veterans' physical wounds, but their illnesses are cancers with mysterious etiologies. Coleman is sent to a psychiatrist when his cancer is declared inoperable, leading him to remark, "So, I have a psychosomatic cancer?" In another context his words might be heard as a good-natured quip tossed to nurses as he is wheeled out of the ward. But in this film, "psychosomatic" is more functional, creating the mind–body, cause-effect tangle known as a "conversion disorder" that the filmmakers want introduced to viewers.

In her 1997 book *Hystories: Hysterical Epidemics and Modern Media* literature professor Elaine Showalter wrote about conversion disorders in war veterans as the way in which mind–body interplay can convert mental stress into physical, bodily symptoms. The symptoms presented are real but rooted in unexpressed psychological problems, not physical injury from exploding shells and chemicals. In other words, the psychological bases of the anxiety, depression, paranoia, and anger that De Victor sees go unrecognized because her gaze is being turned away, redirected to an externality, AO. Just as doctors in WWI mistakenly attributed the paralyses of their patients to exploding shells, De Victor lets AO's emotional potency woo her away from the psychological problems for which her clients need help.[32]

The final lines written for AO's makeover from an herbicide with dangers to human physical health to that of a player in war-trauma diagnostics come when Ritter's character, Frank Coleman, stumbles into the unspeakable—sexual disfunction. Coleman is collecting information on the health of his buddies from Vietnam. We see and hear one of them talking on a pay phone to Coleman. He says his marriage has dissolved and, turning away from a passerby, alludes in a hushed tone to his diminished interest in sex. Later, we hear De Victor asking her clients if they experience numbness in their extremities—one of the classic symptoms of conversion disorders. The exchanges go like this:

De Victor:	You have any health problems since you got back? Numbness in your fingers or hand? Feet? Loss of sex drive? (Pause) Look baby, you don't have to answer, I'm doing a special report.
Vet:	You don't tell anybody, okay? My ol' lady says I come back different. I'm not the same man. I don't know.
De Victor:	... tell me, you ever see the spraying in `Nam ?
Vet:	Why sure ...

Sexual performance is complicated, a blend of physical energies, social channeling, and desires. Desire itself is a fusion of mind and body, emotional, cultural, and biological. But De Victor's linking of the spraying with diminished sexual desire in a cause–effect sequence is reductive. It is the point in the film when AO's place is sealed as a diagnostic factor in the popular perceptions of war trauma.[33]

It may have been AO's reputation as a secret weapon with hard to detect effects on human health that made it a dog whistle for paranoia. The "walking timebomb" in De Victor's office hears voices, the "lost ones," warning him about the VA. Viewers leave those opening frames of *Unnatural Cause*'s with "psychotic" on their minds and that is the theme that is reinforced as life in the wards unfolds:

[Vet #1]:	"... my opinion, they had a list of us over there, a list of guys who weren't supposed to come back. But some of us slipped under the radar ..."
[Vet #2]:	"Paranoid"

[Vet #1]:   "... so now, they gotta track us down and ace-us-out over here—and the VA is in on it."

[Vet #2]:   "Paranoid, a lot of them come back that way, it's the guilt."

In a bed next to the dying Frank Coleman, a veteran declares: "the only thing worse than the VC is the VA."[34]

The film gives us no reason to think De Victor hears the deranged ramblings of the "walking timebomb" and other clients as anything more than symptoms, albeit ones associated with AO—until the office switchboard operator confirms that her phone is being tapped and De Victor is ordered to drop her interest in AO. With those turns, she begins to think that veterans' suspicions that the government betrayed them in Vietnam and is now out to silence them might have validity; phrases like "coverup from top to bottom" and "we got enemies in high places" pepper more of her conversations.

De Victor's implicit validation of her clients' conditions can be viewed as character development—a screenwriting standard—or as political growth, her shedding of naiveté about government. But seen and heard in the movie theaters, the conspricism in those views fed other sentiments, some that lent AO for use as a prop in writing the great American betrayal narrative for the lost war, and some that abetted the victim-veteran identity which displaced from American political culture the memory of antiwar Vietnam veterans.

Literature professor Showalter warns about the paranoia at work in medical and psychiatric settings which use "conspiracy theories to explain every unidentified symptom and syndrome." Extending the reach of "conversion disorder," she is averring that psychological illness can manifest as political sentiment that diverts attention from the ailments, the "real villains" in her words, that cry out for treatment. She quotes anthropologist Sherril Mulhern as saying the emergence of conspiracy theory has become a "consistent pattern" in the American clinical setting where "a growing, socially operative conspiratorial mentality [is] undermining crucial sectors of the mental health ... system."[35]

By its ending, *Unnatural Causes* had created an allegoric AO with as much political and cultural significance as its chemical and biological properties. Edwin Martini's characterization of it as "social disease" captured its fit with the PTSD that psychiatrist Robert Fleming anticipated in 1985 to be better understood as "sociosis" than neurosis, more societal in nature than psychological.

Unnatural Causes may or may not have had an impact like *Rambo's* on the psychiatrists crafting the diagnostic nomenclature of PTSD. But the new Diagnostic and Statistical Manual, DSM III, which came out two years later, included PTSD, legitimating it for professional use. Two decades into the twenty-first century, the spectacle-making power of veterans with a silent killer in their bodies having fathered deformed babies and, now grandchildren, continues to draw the attention of historians and antiwar activists to humanitarian themes lingering from the war in Vietnam.

Meanwhile, new generations of GIs, Marines, sailors, and airmen deploy for twenty-first century wars expecting to come home, like their elders did from Vietnam, with unseen wounds that include damage from chemical and biological weaponry. Enemies like the Iraqi Saddam Hussein are sometimes rumored to possess those weapons, but it is the "friendly fire" from their own uranium-tipped rounds and the burn-pit emissions on their own bases of unidentified residues that send personnel home feeling sick—and suspicious that their own government is responsible for their hard-to-diagnose ailments. The paranoia nascent in those suspicions, spelling PTSD to journalists and liberal academics, is one of AO's most pernicious legacies.[36]

AO's enhancement of victim-veteran imagery fed public upset that the losses in Vietnam were more than military. As political code, it dovetailed neatly with presidential candidate Jimmy Carter's assertion in 1977 that the war's destruction was *mutually* costly to the United States and Vietnam. It was Carter's mawkish reading of history that licensed the United States to continue the war indefinitely by economic sanctions and political isolation and lodged the experience as collective trauma in American memory.[37]

Mythical or not, the strong America perceived to have been lost in Vietnam was real enough to voters 50 years later to elect Donald Trump as president on the campaign slogan, Make America Great Again.

Notes

1 Rieckhoff, *Big Think*.
2 In her own credit to helicopters for the "historical focus" they provide for American memory of the war, Eastman, *The American War in Vietnam*, 77 cites Biedler's "The Last Huey" for recognizing that helicopters are second only to the Veteran's Memorial wall on the capitol mall "constructing a history out of the twinned resources of memory and imagination." '
3 Zierler, *The Invention of Ecocide*, 10.
4 Martini, *Agent Orange*, 212.
5 The American public initially believed that Strategic Hamlets were a way to gather Vietnamese peasants into planned compounds for their protection from Viet Cong terrorism. Only later did it become clear that they were a way to separate peasants sympathetic to the VC in order to deprive the guerrillas of material and political support. Still later scholarship (Catton, *Diem's Final Failure*; Taylor, *Fragments of the Present*) revealed the role of the Hamlets in depopulating the countryside as tactic in the modernization of Vietnam (i.e. urbanization).
6 Louis Hacker. "A Testament of Faith in Man and His Capacity for Growth." *The New York Times*, December 29, 1957.
7 Zierler, *The Invention of Ecocide*, 89 calls Commoner the "'father' of modern environmentalism," and 152 says Gaylord Nelson "founded Earth Day."
8 Rozanne Junker, 2020. Correspondence, April 23.
9 The search of the *New York Times* archive was done in 2020 by Jennifer Whelan, librarian at the College of the Holy Cross.
10 Thiele, *Environmentalism for a New Millennium: The Challenge of Coevolution*, 12.
11 The Webinar was moderated by Paul Shannon from the American Friends Service Committee, one of the frontline antiwar organizations during the war in Vietnam that all but dropped out of sight as environmentalism and a host of other liberal causes

poached energy from the antiwar movement in the post-war years. Gary Butterfield was the featured guest. Butterfield declared conscientious objector status after being drafted for the war in Vietnam and was in 2022 on the Veteran's for Peace Climate Crisis & Militarism Project.

12 Klare, "Saying Goodbye to The Planet Earth," *tomdispatch.com* May 23, 2022.

13 Young, M., *The Vietnam Wars*, 255.

14 Hunt, *The Turning*, 35–36.

15 My phrase "absence with its own presence" is adapted from Eastman's, *The American War in Vietnam*, 10, idea of the "present absence."

16 Young, M., *The Vietnam Wars,* 34. Dioxin according to Zeirler, *The Invention of Ecocide,* 6, "is short for 2,3,7,8-tetrachlorodibenzo-para-dioxin or TCDD."

17 Young, M., Ibid., 34.

18 Ibid., 37–38.

19 Wilcox, *Scorched Earth*, 11–12, 25–40.

20 Zierler, *The Invention of Ecocide*, 8.

21 Martini, *Agent Orange*, 171.

22 Ibid., 177.

23 Ibid., 175.

24 The Purple Heart is not awarded for AO claims. See "Common Myths about The Purple Heart Medal" (www.americanwarlibrary.com/theheart.htm).

25 Vietnam veteran Barry Romo (2019, p. 10) was active in AO issues in the 1970s and remembers, "… the guy from the anti-abortion group—Randal Terry from Operation Rescue—would show up … They were there to demand that people with AO not have abortions."

26 The WBBM broadcast is unavailable to the author. The description use here is the Kurtis quote is from Martini, p. 155.

27 Young, M., *The Vietnam Wars*, 40.

28 Martini, *Agent Orange*, 158.

29 In their 1994 *Vietnam War Films*, now considered the "bible" of the war's filmography, authors Jean-Jacques Malo and Tony Williams remark that AO "has hardly been touch by filmmakers; only two feature films were devoted to it, both TV movies: Lamont Johnson's *Unnatural Causes* in 1986 and Bleckner's *My Father* in 1988." Both films were backgrounded by the war itself but use military operations solely to contextualize the post-war maladies of American veterans

30 Hoge, "Navigating the Transition from Combat to Home," 38.

31 The movie garnered a Golden Globe nomination as did Ritter. Woodward won an Emmy nomination for her portrayal of De Victor.

32 Showalter, *Hysteries*, 13.

33 See Best and Kellner, *Postmodern Theory*, 86–97, on desire.

34 VC are the letters for Viet Cong itself American slang for the Vietnamese Communist military organization, more properly name The National Liberation Front.

35 Showalter, *Hystories*, 26–27.

36 See Megan K. Stack, "The Monster That Followed Him Home from War." *New York Times*, March 25, 2022.

37 See Appy, *American Reckoning*, 229, on Carter's statement and its consequences. Historian George Herring described the war in Vietnam as the "unending" war. Martini and Allen, *Until the Last Man Comes Home*, have good accounts of "war of other means" waged against Vietnam long after the guns went silent. See Hagopian, *The Vietnam War in American Memory*.

5

TRAUMATIC BRAIN INJURY

From News to Nomenclature

> In veterans of the Iraq war, post-concussive symptoms have been more strongly correlated with PTSD and depression than with concussion.
>
> (Dr. Charles Hoge)

Dr. Charles Hoge was writing about traumatic brain injury (TBI) and war veterans in a 2009 *New England Journal of Medicine* article. He went on to say that "psychological factors, compensation and litigation, and patients' expectations are strong predictors of the persistence of [TBI] symptoms." Combat experience was conspicuously absent from his list of items that would predict whether a veteran was likely to have TBI. On the other hand, included in the "patients' expectations" of which he spoke, were the "widespread use of the terms 'signature injury,' 'invisible wound,' and 'silent epidemic'," all arising out of the news reports on troops home from Iraq, not the professional mental health literature.[1]

Hoge is the foremost American researcher on TBI and readers now familiar with the history of war trauma treatment would not have been surprised by his report that veterans with no evidence of concussion could be more likely to have a diagnosis of brain injury than those who do. Afterall, as far back as World War I doctors saw patients with the symptoms of shellshock who had never been exposed to exploding shells. Some doctors wondered if their patients might be faking their injuries to gain compensation. It was a suspicion that went back decades to the first railway accidents that produced novel injuries claimed by men who had never been near a train. At the time, newly founded insurance policies covering train accidents raised questions about the motivations of claimants—were they making-up their injuries to collect insurance? Known as "railway spine," those symptoms were later understood as

DOI: 10.4324/9781003391906-6

instances of "male hysteria," a forerunner to shellshock.[2] But not all physicians thought that pretending for compensation was the right explanation. Rather, patients just might not remember or understand when and why they got the hurts they suffered. Sigmund Freud had noticed that women treated for hysteria could not always remember when their symptoms first appeared. It was as if that memory had been "put away" to where it would not be a bother. Pierre Janet, a contemporary of Freud, distinguished between traumatic and narrative memory and coined the term "subconscious" where unpleasant experiences could be "stored."

Hysteria continued to influence approaches to shellshock. Thanks to the theatrics and photographs created by Jean Martin Charcot at Salpêtrière Hospital in Paris, hysteria had a "grip on the sympathy and imagination of the public," as Historian Martin Stone put it, before which doctors themselves were "well-nigh helpless."[3] Hysteria's tendency, however, was to gender the diagnostic issues: hysteria was considered a female disorder, something psychological, something for which something-about-the-patients-themselves was responsible for their symptoms. Doctors, who were mostly men, were reluctant to take war veterans down that path—"anything but psychological," as historian Elaine Showalter said.[4] Neurology offered a way out. Perhaps the symptoms observed as hysteria were caused by something physical—not psychological. There were ancient notions that physiological instabilities could unsettle the mind. Nineteenth-century neurologists thought that brain lesions might be the cause of mental abnormalities, but autopsies of patients treated for hysteria failed to reveal any lesions.

Internal or external? Mind or brain? Physical or psychic? Psychological or cultural? Material or imaginative? W.H. Rivers tried to dissolve the dichotomies. Following Freud's cue, he concluded that it was WWI veterans' fantasies of the martial experiences they thought were expected of them that came out as false memories of those things having happened. Those false memories, then, generated the physical symptoms of shellshock—and imagined the exploding shells responsible for the symptoms.[5]

The Freudian assignment of causation for physical ailments to the decidedly non-physical realm of the subconscious reversed the more typical, and even commonsensical understanding that injury to the body could weigh on the mind and be emotionally upsetting and unnerving. But the idea that soldiers, the standard-bears of manhood, could be brought down by something other than the enemy's weapons was unthinkable; the idea that that "something" could lie within the wounded veteran himself was unimaginable.

World War II: A Different War, Different Representations

World War II was a bit of an interlude in the professional tussles over war trauma. The psychiatric causality rate for American soldiers was high, about 20% of all casualties. But the intensity of fighting at the D-Day landings on Frances's

Normandy beach and bloody Tarawa in the Pacific, where 1,500 marines died and 2,000 more wounded in three days, left little room for wonder about why some veterans were left mute, shaky, or paralytic by their experiences. The causes for which the lives and limbs had been taken were, moreover, widely viewed as legitimate, even righteous—Nazi death camps had been liberated, and the Japanese bombing of Pearl Harbor avenged. And the war had been won, all but precluding the negative energies of blame and guilt that nettled the post-wars of WWI and would shadow the war in Vietnam into the twenty-first century.

Recovery treatments were filmed for the US Army by John Huston already known for his 1941 films *Maltese Falcon* and *High Sierra* that made actor Humphrey Bogart famous. His documentary footage was later turned into *Let There be Light*, a film suppressed by the Army until 1981 out of concern that its depiction of wounded psyches might hurt recruitment efforts. The film's references to shellshock indicate that healthcare professionals were approaching their casualties from the Second World War with the First World War very much on their minds. In the film, we see the "talking therapy" in practice, the approach to mental disorders associated with psychoanalysis. The narrator says the approach draws "no sharp lines between mind and body." An arm or leg might be paralyzed "as if caused by a spinal lesion," he says, "but it is purely psychological."

The narrator explains that these men had grown up "educated to hate war" but were then thrust into it and expected to perform as soldiers. Patients' class backgrounds, their parents' own inarticulateness, limited their ability to express their fears and anxieties, so their memories of combat, too painful to live with, were banished to their subconscious. Once the attending psychiatrist coxed that memory from the patient, sometimes with the help of hypnosis, he was relieved of his physical symptoms. Veterans with doubts about their personal strength of character were assured that their responses were normal, that anyone having experienced the horrors they did would feel the same way.

The Freudian hunch that veterans' physical symptoms were body-speak for personal discomforts with war that John Huston brought to the screen did not sit well with critics. Its speculation that some men's' inner-Audie Murphy might be tempered by the Sixth Commandment was unsettling; the specter of pacifism wraithing through the ranks a nightmare for the military brass. More practically, the images of men left mentally enfeebled by war would make it hard to recruit a new generation of troops. Fearing its public impact, the Army ordered *Let There Be Light* banned from theaters wherein it would not be seen again until 1981.[6]

Huston took his punches for the film. When it came out in 1946, fears of communism born with the 1917 Russian Revolution had been muted by the alliance formed by the United States and Soviet Union against Hitler. But the culmination of the Chinese Communist Revolution in 1949, rekindled those fears, and they would grow into a hysteria during the Cold War years of the 1950s. Worries that the mettle to staunch the Red Tide might not be found in American men, as hinted by Huston's *Let There Be Light*, put a target on the film's market and his back. After joining other Hollywood artists to form the "Committee for the First Amendment" for protection from government prosecution for un-American activities, Huston decamped to Ireland in 1952.

Psychoanalysis, meanwhile, was poised for a drop in professional standing. It had come out of the WWII years highly regarded for its insights into the authoritarian personalities that enabled the rise of European fascism, insights that, as well, diminished chances that that awful period would be repeated. During and after the war, Frankfurt School Marxists, schooled in Freud, fled Nazism for the United States where they staked a redoubt for psychoanalysis at the New School for Social Research in New York City. By the end of the 1950s, however, conservative winds were sweeping into American intellectual life, fostering a positivist "scientism" that was hostile to the interpretive approaches to social life taken by Freudians. Those winds began to be felt in the country's response to the war in Korea, 1950–1953.[7]

Korea and the Return of Spectacle

If Americans remember the war in Korea at all it is as their "forgotten war." Overshadowed by "The Good Fight," as the Second World War would be remembered, and "The Greatest Generation" that fought it, the Korean War suffered the status deprivation of neglected progeny, the unwanted offspring of the *real* wars that had preceded it, World Wars I and II. It did not help, either, that Korea was never declared an *actual* war, so it *actually* never ended. But forgetting something is always about what is remembered in its place. Seemingly in anticipation of journalist Tom Engelhardt's insight into why trauma-stricken veterans became the proximate figures for remembering the war in Vietnam— "Honor the Veteran, Forget the War," as he put it—the war in Korea itself would be displaced in popular memory by the images of its veterans, the prisoners of war (POWs) brainwashed by their communist captors.

The notion of "brainwash" provided an answer to the great dichotomies bedeviling the diagnoses of war trauma since WWI: Was it a mind or brain problem? Brain? Physical or psychic? The brain is *physical*, washing is *physical*. Internal or external? External, the wash*er* is external to the brain being washed. Material or imaginative? A thoroughly material model. But psychological or cultural? Brainwashing allegedly *washes* away the personalities and political values of its victims. The washed brains are blank slates upon which new cultural traits can be written. Of course, the target of brainwashing was mind control but the physicality of brains being washed had the same conjuring power that "lightening in a jar" had to excite sixteenth-century imaginations about electricity (Chapter 1). The brainwashing imagery seeded a brain-to-mind paradigm for understanding war trauma that would gestate in the nomenclature of PTSD and burst into full bloom with TBI during the war in Iraq.

The opportunity to "show" a brain being washed, or at least show the behavior said to be left by a brain wash, was a call to Hollywood that would not go unanswered. When 21 POWs chose to stay in Korea rather than return home after their release, Cold War shivers ran down the cultural spine of America. Had the absence from homelife of fathers serving in the military during WWII deprived boys of role models for manhood? Had the affluence of the expanding postwar economy already corroded traditional values of loyalty and dedication to service? Did the turncoats in Korea portend future generations of softies unable, or god forbid, unwilling to meet the challenge of international communism? The America threatened by mind-snatching communist brainwashers on the outside and the erosion of character by material comforts on the inside was subject matter just waiting for the Big Screen.

Cold War anxieties drove ticket buyers to the box offices where Korean War POWs were portrayed as men-of-weak-character whose shortcomings resulted from a materialistic and permissive society at home. *The Rack* (1956) and *The Manchurian Candidate* (1962) vivified the brain as the battle site where the hidden injuries of war were registered and infused the public perception of war trauma with the sex and gender themes that would become a staple in the PTSD literature.

In *The Rack* (1956), Paul Newman played Army Captain Ed Hall Jr. Hall had been captured and held by the communists for two years and is now court martialed for "aid and comfort to the enemy." Under questioning, Hall admits to having made propaganda statements demanded by his communist captors and acknowledges he suffered no torture prior to doing so. His defense attorney then asks Hall to recall the prison interrogations and how the communists preyed on the details of his childhood insecurities left by his parents. Hall's mother had died when he was young and his father, a career military man, left him in the care of a housekeeper. Growing up in a cold, unloving environment, Hall developed a mama's boy personality that sought acceptance by pleasing parental figures. The prosecuting attorney summed-up the case against Hall: "the Chinese found your weakness, a very lonely boy—they beat you with it."[8]

The Manchurian Candidate, one of the great spectacles in the history of film, followed in 1962. In it, Staff Sgt. Raymond Shaw is captured in Korea. He is programmed by the Chinese to carry out an assassination plot in the United States after he returns home from the war. Shaw's domineering mother (Angela Lansbury) is part of the plot; Shaw is portrayed as too weak—incestuously so—to disobey her. His mother's husband, who is running for president, is Shaw's target for assassination. Major Bennett Marco (Frank Sinatra), who had been captured with Shaw and remains unsettled by the experience, has an inkling of something untoward afoot and races to the campaign rally in Madison Square Garden to stop Shaw.

The Battle of Paradigms Resumed: Neurology vs. Psychiatry

The support for World War II on the home front, the feel-good reception home that veterans received, and the relative ease with which they slid back into the expanding economy meant that their war-born troubles, whatever they were, were not a public preoccupation going into the 1950s; nor did veterans' postwar adjustments restart the post-World War I debate between neurologists and psychiatrists over what war trauma was and wasn't. The brainwashing imagery spawned by the Korean War POW storyline, however, courted professional endorsement from the neurologists. Their approval was encouraged by the ease with which the indoctrination narrative was adopted by popular culture: that "skilled communist indoctrinators had brainwashed American soldiers into renouncing their country" became, wrote historian Craig Howes, "the essence of received opinion." Perhaps it was that hegemonic common-sense-ness of brainwashing that kept professional pugilism over war trauma abeyant going in the Viet Nam War years.[9]

Debates over war trauma resumed in the wake of the war in Vietnam. Mostly skipping over Korea and World War II, discussions leap-frogged back to World War I to frame analogies to shellshock—the unseen hurts of Vietnam veterans were like shellshock—with little recognition that shellshock had gone into medical history as a discredited notion. The inclusion of PTSD in DSM III did little to quiet the debates.[10]

As a diagnostic tool, PTSD was stalked by empirical incongruities similar to those bedeviling shellshock—psychiatric casualties in Vietnam had been more common among non-combat troops than combat. Only 15% of men in Vietnam saw combat whereas news sources regularly reported that 30–50% of Vietnam veterans suffer from PTSD. Flashbacks, the *sine qua non* of PTSD, became the touchstone of professional disagreement. Reprising Janet's distinction between traumatic and narrative memory, the neurological premise is that there is something physiological about flashbacks, the "soft" version believing that combat-appropriate behavior like hitting-the-deck when hearing a shot fired involve neurotransmitters sending signals along familiar paths to tell the body what do.[11]

The harder version developed by Dr. Bessel van der Kolk imagined the subconscious physiologically and posited stress extreme enough to increase the size of the locus (sir) coeruleus pathways to the limbic system—a physical change that could support abnormal responses to war-like stimuli. However, a study reported by Ruth Leys in her book *Trauma: A Genealogy*, compared Vietnam veterans with and without a PTSD diagnosis and found no difference in their bio-chemical responses when they were exposed to combat-like stimuli.[12] "Many mental health experts believe," wrote James Dao for *The New York Times* in 2013, that the search for something physical with a causal connection to PTSD, "is futile." He could also have said it is basically brain-lesion theory in new clothes.[13]

The "soft" version of flashbacks as re-experienced habituated response is even more difficult to sustain. First, of all, there is little in military training or combat experience that is repeated often enough to become "habit." Second, the empirical evidence for anyone "hitting the deck" from, say, firecrackers is as convincing as the "hippy chick" spitting on returnees from Vietnam at San Francisco Airport. Folklore is the player here—flashbacks as a form of narrative memory. Or as psychiatrist Fred Frankel, an early skeptic of neurological models for PTSD wrote, "Flashbacks are as likely a product of imagination as memory."[14] A 1983 article in the *American Journal of Psychiatry* examined five cases whereupon men had presented post-Vietnam War symptoms. Three of the men said they were former POWs. "In fact," the authors found, "none had been prisoners of war, four (of the five) had never been in Vietnam, and two had never even been in the military."[15]

The more intriguing challenge to the brain-trauma paradigm comes from neurologist Suzanne O'Sullivan who cited PTSD as an example of "looping," the feedback effect of societal expectations on patients and doctors. O'Sullivan references philosopher Ian Hacking's description of looping as "making up people," the process of changing a person's identity by classifying them psychiatrically. The labels used for classifications are derived from societal contexts, she says. The cases of "Havana Syndrome," for example, show how "societal pressure created a medical drive to explain [psychological symptoms] in a biological way." The Havana story unfolded in 2017 when state department employees in Cuba complained of dizziness, tinnitus, fatigue, headaches, and hearing loss. The first inquiry into the symptoms called them "a unique constellation ... 'a complex brain network disorder' consistent with a 'traumatic brain injury'—but without any history of brain trauma."[16] The "societal pressure" for a TBI-like diagnosis in this case was, she avers, to create an appearance that Russian surveillance technology operating in Havana created brain damage, an impression that made the specter of Russian stealth more real for Americans.[17]

But brain lesions are still in the fight. Brain matters are physiological and injuries to the brain imply external events having occurred *to* the victim/patient—like those exploding shells causing shellshock. But how can something as definitionally physical like "brain injury" be made to look and sound like it belongs in a collection of purely psychological and emotional categories? *Viola*—the discursive conjunction formed by adding the word "traumatic" to "brain injury." This gives us a new phrase that says what? That brain injury *is* traumatic, would be redundant. Rather, it infers a distinction between concussion-caused brain injury and trauma-caused brain injury. Which, read in reverse, infers a distinction between the girly, psychological, hysteria-type trauma, and *real* trauma—a manly physiological type that leaves markings in flesh, blood, and tissue. With "traumatic *brain injury*" mixed in, the PTSD package now becomes organic, nominally biological, relieving it of the stigma— "only psychological."

The Central Park Jogger and NFL Quarterbacks: Rehearsing for TBI in War Trauma

Like PTSD and Shellshock before it, TBI gained standing in medical science through news reports and popular culture. There were only a few references to TBI in medical journals until the end of the 1980s. A 1988 article in the journal *Brain Injury* noted research on TBI to be "so sparse" that the author had to "extrapolate" from other material to write about it. Professional journals at the time seldom made connections between brain injury and psychological and psychiatric conditions, aka trauma.[18] And when the connections began to be made, they came from a sensational crime story that morphed through the news media into a mental health story.

The Central Park Jogger. The first *New York Times* reference to TBI came in 1983. The next six years averaged only about one more per year, and almost always used with the lower-case spelling. In 1987 there were no TBI stories in the *Times* and only one in 1988. None of them mentioned war veterans.

Public awareness of TBI picked up on May 21, 1989, with the news that a 28-year-old white investment banker had been beaten and raped a month before while jogging in New York City's Central Park. The victim, left comatose and unidentified, was later unable to remember what had happened to her or identify her assailants. After six weeks at the city's Metropolitan Hospital, she was moved to Gaylord Hospital in Wallingford, Connecticut for therapy and recovery. According to *Newsweek* reporters David Gelman and Elizabeth Ann Leonard, she was told at that time what had happened, although the *Newsweek* story did not say what she told or who told her.

The quick identification of the attackers as young male members of minority groups, and the anonymity of the comatose victim—dubbed "The Central Park Jogger" by the media—invited a could-have-been-me public identity with the story. By December 1989, the *New York Times* had run 18 stories on the Jogger, many with references to TBI; for thousands of readers, including healthcare professionals, the stories were their first exposure to that idea. With nothing intrinsic about the event itself or mental health science having changed—except the *Times*'s framing of its stories—the news narrative of the Jogger began evolving from a story about crime to a story about mental health. At issue was the Jogger's memory: unable to remember the attack, she could neither confirm nor rebut the identities of the five young men tired for it, a lapse that their defense attorney averred might have been strategic; with the Jogger unable to say that the five men charged were *not* the ones who attacked her, they were convicted.[19]

The launching of TBI into popular and professional prominence by The Jogger story in the 1990s raises two questions: Why was an obscure idea like TBI, not yet even a diagnostic category, unknown even to mental health practitioners at the time, of greater interest than a criminal case loaded with the sex/gender/race storylines, usually catnip for journalists, screenwriters, and sociologists? And why then? The answer to the first is actually in the premise of the question itself—the attraction of the unknown, the same magnetism that enchanted salon-goers in the 1500s. The workings of the brain were unseen, sensually intangible, mysterious, an invitation to the imagination. Crime, race, class, gender? All empirically accessible, measurable—not so interesting.

Quarterbacks with Head Injuries. Along with the jogger story, TBI faded from the news in the mid-1990s. It returned in 1997 following the path laid by the jogger case from an off-topic spectacle—professional football in this case—that ended on the playing field of medical discourse. The first of those stories came on July 16 after injuries to high-profile quarterbacks Steve Young of the San Francisco '49ers and Troy Aikman of the Dallas Cowboys had led the National Football League to begin a five-year study of players suffering concussions. The story reported that the League would add neurological and psychological testing to its evaluation of players. With sports as a hook, TBI was back in play.

The emotional and cultural properties of the quarterback story outweighed whatever it said about the physical health of the players involved. Quarterbacks are the best protected and least hit of any players on the field. Subsequent inquiries into the long-term impact of repeated hits to the head and something called chronic traumatic encephalopathy (CTE) drew professional and fan interest during the twenty-teen years but they, too, proved little.[20] The more obvious damage left by careers in football was *body weight*. An epidemic of obesity growing since the 1970s was reported 22 years later in a 2019 *New York Times* story: The National Football League's "emphasis on the passing game and quarterback protection has led teams to stock their offensive and defensive lines with ever-larger men, some of them weighing well over 300 pounds." "Blocking for $25-million-a-year quarterbacks," read the story, "can put linemen in [a] high risk category … for diabetes, hypertension, and cardiac problems."[21]

The deadly body weight hung on 300-pounders whose names were tossed off in descriptions of a "missed blocking assignment" went unnoticed, while a quarterback's needle-threading 40-yard pass proclaimed "spectacular!" by the play-booth announcer would be replayed *ad nauseum* by sportscasters the following week. It was the entertainment value of their passes that made quarterbacks props, spectacles associable with commercial products and, no less, a new diagnostic category searching for scientific recognition and a market.

Given the visibility of behemoth football linemen and the measurable danger of the weight they carried, it is somewhat ironic that it was conjecture about a *hidden* injury—that to the brain and mind of quarterbacks—that piqued public interest. The cultural accruements of quarterbacks no doubt added to their off-field media appeal. As with the Jogger, depicted in the newspapers as "a star with a bright future—smart, young, rich, and white," a list of traits inviting an appended "beautiful,"[22] Aikman and Young were as handsome as could be. But as it was with male hysteria in the nineteenth century, shellshock in World War I, and

PTSD after Vietnam, it was the lure of the unknown, the mysteries of the mind, magnified by the terror of the *injured* mind, that fixed TBI in the minds of news reporters about to cover the new wars in the Middle East.

Recipe for Spectacle: A War Reporter with a War Injury

On February 27, 2007, ABC News aired a documentary "To Iraq and Back" that was based on a book written by Bob Woodruff, its newscaster who had been wounded while covering the war in Iraq in 2006. Woodruff was already in the spotlight as the successor to Peter Jennings, the immensely popular newsman who had recently died of cancer. On assignment to Iraq, Woodruff had suffered wounds to the head by an improvised explosive device (IED). With his telegenic looks wounded on a military convoy, the story of his recovery would galvanize the public's emotions about war trauma. The *New York Times* gave it front-page coverage; the *Times* and *Washington Post* covered it for days thereafter. A year later, Woodruff's book about his hospitalization and recovery was a *Times* best seller having bumped Barack Obama's autobiography *Audacity of Hope* from the top of the list.

Co-authored with his wife Lee, the book virtually constructed the distinction between just-PTSD and *his* TBI. Despite the absence of TBI in medical journals up to that point, TBI emerged from the news conference as the disorder he struggled to overcome. The *New York Times* report on the news conference mentioned TBI four times; in the month after, nine *Times* stories connected TBI with war veterans. The most important of the nine was General Paul Eaton's March 6 op-ed in which he declared TBI to be "the signature malady of the [Iraq] war." Within weeks, news organizations across the country had adopted the phrase. Medical science followed: prior to the ABC broadcast only one journal connected war injury and TBI; in 2008 there were 12 and that number grew to over 50 in a few months.[23] The legitimating source for the very existence of this new diagnostic category? Woodruff's own book. The galvanizing visual of TBI's existence? The spectacle of Woodruff's now-distended face.

Two months after the ABC Special on Bob Woodruff's book, *Washington Post* reporter Ronald Glasser declared IEDs to be "the signature *weapon*" of the war. According to Glasser, "Iraq has brought back one of the worst afflictions of World War I: shellshock. The brain of the soldiers is shocked, truly."[24] He quoted a neurologist Stephen Macedo saying, "When the sound wave moves through the brain, it seems to cause little gas bubbles to form … when they pop, it leaves a cavity. So, you are littering people's brains with these little holes."[25]

The science-fiction quality to that description reimagines the legendary lesions of medical lore. Advances in computer technology that made CT and CAT brain scans possible, so-called functional MRIs, or fMRIs, were not much help. Searching for physiological evidence for TBI, Dr. Michael Weiner, UC Professor of radiology and psychiatry and Director of the VA Center for

Imaging Neurogenerative Diseases reported his brain scans "show[ing] nothing." A 2016 study by the National Academy of Sciences found false positives in fMRI data up to 70% of the time. The finding, wrote *New York Times* reporter Kate Murphy, encouraged critics' dismissal of fMRIs as "nothing more than a high-tech phrenology," the junk science popularized by the German anatomist Franz Joseph Gall in the 1700s.[26]

TBI, moreover, was surrounded by the same sort of empirical issues that raised skepticism about shellshock and PTSD. In Iraq in 2007 there were 3,000 TBI injuries and 117 deaths attributed to IED explosions—an impossible of ratio of 25–1 given that the Humvee vehicles targeted by the IEDs were crewed by only 4 or 5 men. If one of the five was killed, how could 25 have sustained brain injuries?

But the power of lesions-as-legend might override their low standing in medical science. For a 2012 *New York Times* column, Nicholas Kristoff wrote about Iraq War veteran Ken Richards who is being treated for PTSD and TBI, reporting that lesions had been found in his brain.[27]

Let's return to Dr. Charles Hoge's observation that a PTSD diagnosis is a better predictor of TBI than a concussion, and ask again, "How that can be?" The answer in short-form is that veterans having suffered brain damage from a concussion have the Purple Heart for combat-validation and the service-connected health benefits that come with it—they don't need the TBI diagnosis to buff-up a PTSD claim. But PTSD itself does not qualify for a Purple Heart. Veterans seeking recognition for their PTSD claim, *sans* a Purple Heart, reach for the recognition of their "hidden injury," the "unseen wound" of their TBI. Additionally, the presumptive physiological nature of TBI functions to credential the combat bona fides of the veteran.[28]

Put more sociologically, the answer to the question posed by Hoge is that societal norms surrounding men, masculinity, and war, combine with the public imaginations of combat experience, and the vulnerability of medical science to the images of war trauma in popular culture, to conjure physical and external causes of effects that are internal and physiological. To bumper-sticker it: The PTSD diagnosis *calls forth* TBI as the credentialing condition to justify PTSD itself.

The May 24, 2014, *The New York Times* Sunday Magazine featured the work of neurologist van der Kolk in bringing new approaches in brain study to bear on PTSD and veterans. In the article, van der Kolk uses as an example "the guy at the end of [the 2008 film] 'The Hurt Locker'" as "incapable of playing with his kid," attributing that insensitivity "to brain damage wrought by the traumatic stress of combat." Having referred in writing to the same storyline in the film to make a different point, I wrote the following letter-to-the-editor of Magazine:

> Could be [brain damage]. But it could also be that, like [I saw] the character in the film, some men find dishes and diapers on the home front more threatening

than unexploded bombs at the battlefront; and that PTSD is better understood through the sociological studies of family and the cultural studies of masculinity than the neuro-speak given it by brain physiologists.[29]

Notes

1 Hoge et al. "Care of War Veterans with Mild Traumatic Brain Injury—Flawed Perspectives." *New England Journal of Medicine* 2009 pp. 1588–1591.
2 "Faking impairment," writes Dr. Albert M. Drukteimis, "may not be that difficult." In one study he wrote,

> Children were instructed to "fake bad" on comprehensive neuropsychological testing with minimal guidance on how to do it. Of 42 clinical neuropsychologists who reviewed these cases, 93 percent diagnosed abnormality, 87 percent of those said it was because of brain dysfunction; no clinician detected malingering. When specific tests for malingering or exaggeration are not administered, the likelihood of missing deliberate distortion is even higher.

3 Stone, "Shellshock and the Psychologists," 254.
4 Showalter as spoken in *Science Odyssey: In Search of Ourselves*" for Public Television.
5 Harrington, *The Cure Within*, 75–76, has an accessible account of Freud's breakthrough. See also Stone, "Shellshock and the Psychologists," 255 for Rivers' reworking of Freud's insights. *New York Times* columnist Maureen Down "Wishes as Lies" made clever use of Freud's insight in writing about Connecticut Attorney General Richard Blumenthal's false claim to being a Vietnam veteran.
6 Audie Murphy is said to have been the most decorated soldier in WWII for his heroics at Anzio in Italy. Huston would base a character for the 1962 film *Red Badge of Courage* on Murphy.
7 Chancer and Andrews, *The Unhappy Divorce of Sociology and Psychoanalysis.*
8 *Time Limit* opened a year later set in a cold and dispirited POW camp where Major Cargill has been brainwashed by the communists. Cargill, played by the star Richard Basehart, is lecturing to his fellow prisoners about Marxism. We then see him stateside in being court-martialed for collaboration.
9 Howes, *Voices of the Vietnam POWs*, 78.
10 The fallacious analogy that PTSD was like shellshock led to the inevitable tautology that shellshock is like PTSD. Writing on August 3, 2014, about World War I poet and resister Siegfried Sassoon, the *New York Times* writer Alan Cowell recalled that authorities sent Sassoon "to be treated for shellshock as post-traumatic stress disorder was then known."
11 I critiqued the flashback/hit-the-deck stories at *CounterPunch.com* (Lembcke, "Flashbacks, Fireworks ... and Cars that Backfire?" Spike Lee, nevertheless, worked a seriously intentioned but cartoonish version of them into his 2020 film *Da Five Bloods.*
12 Leys, *Trauma*, 257–258.
13 Dao, "Study Seeks Biomarkers for Invisible War Scars."
14 Frankel, "The Concept of Flashbacks in Historical Perspective," 321.
15 See the references to "factitious PTSD" in Chapter 4.
16 O'Sullivan, *The Sleeping Beauties*, 157–158.
17 Ibid., 165–177.
18 A Medline search for articles on TBI found only 11 articles in psychiatric and psychology journals before 1988.
19 There is reason to wonder if the discourse switch from crime-to-trauma might have had a strategic angle. In her 2003 memoir *I am the Central Park Jogger*, 196 Meili recounts defense attorney Colin Moore's sardonic quip that "making sure [her] memory is

restored" would enable her to "identify those people who committed the crime," and that "up to the present time, [she has] not sought a memory reconstruction."

20 Belson, "Top Concussion Panel Dismisses Links to C.T.E."

21 Belson, "The NFL's Other Scourge: Obesity"; Belson, "Cheers Fade, The Pain Grows."

22 Burns, *The Central Park Five*, 66.

23 Eaton, "Casualties of the War Budget."

24 Glasser. "A Shock Wave of Brain Injuries." The IEDs, Glasser wrote, had caused "wounds and *even deaths* among troops who have no external signs of trauma but whose brains have been severely damaged" (italics added).

25 An "air embolism" or "gas embolism" entering the brain through blood (the vascular system) is possible but that does not seem to be what Glasser and Macedo have in mind when they write of "sound waves" entering the brain.

   O'Sullivan, *Sleeping Beauties*, 168, expresses similar skepticism about cases of Havana Syndrome in which air bubbles in arteries in brains would "create sound" in alleged victims.

26 Weiner is quoted by Conn Hallinan in "The Brain Trauma Vets: An Epidemic of Psychological Wounds" at *Counter Punch*, June 7, 2008. Murphy "Do You Believe in God? Or Is That a Software Glitch?" Professor of Mathematical Science, Rebecca Goldin and Cindy Merrick expressed their reservations about fMRI in a 2012 article, "Neuroscience or Neurobabble?: What's this thing called fMRI?".

27 Kristoff, "War Wounds."

28 See the *New York Times* editorial "PTSD and the Purple Heart," January 12, 2009.

29 The *Times* did not print my letter.

6

"MORAL INJURY"

Its Own Spectacle

War dehumanizes everyone it touches.

(Gloria Emerson, war reporter)

Not me.

(Jerry Lembcke, author)

Gloria Emerson, famous as a news correspondent during the war in Vietnam, was speaking at the College of the Holy Cross in March 2000. Her appearance was part of a retrospective on the war 25 years after its ending. In her remarks, Emerson noted the awfulness of wars, contending that they dehumanize everyone they touch. The audience was particularly moved by the references to American veterans of the war in Vietnam whose post-war travails she used to illustrate her points.

I was a Holy Cross professor in the audience that evening and Emerson's comments struck a chord with me, as well—but for different reasons. Had there been a Q&A after her talk, I may have taken the mic and said,

Dehumanized by the war in Vietnam? Not me. I came home in February 1970 a better person for having been there. Dehumanized? Not me. If anything, I had *found* my humanity in Vietnam and returned, like thousands of other veterans, with a commitment to help end the war.

Absent that Q&A opportunity, I wrote a note to colleagues the next day in which I acknowledged having seen the terribleness of the war, just as the speaker had described, but I went on to recount the many acts of compassion and generosity

DOI: 10.4324/9781003391906-7

that I had witnessed between Americans and Vietnamese. Today, I would callout the names of Jan Barry, Charlie Clements, Bill Ehrhart, and Chuck Searcy, among many others, who committed their post-war lives to writing, teaching, and service projects devoted to peace.[1]

"Moral Injury": War-Trauma de Jour

Had the phrase "moral injury" been popular in 2000, Gloria Emerson would probably have used it instead of "dehumanized" to describe the effects of war on veterans. Like traumatic brain Injury (TBI), however, it was just gaining recognition at the turn of the millennium, and, like TBI, it had gestated outside of mental health science. Alice Lynn and Staughton Lynd credit Jonathon Shay with being "the first person to use the term 'moral injury' to describe the reactions of Vietnam veterans to atrocities committed in Vietnam." Shay was a psychiatrist who treated Vietnam veterans at the VA hospital in Boston; he developed the term moral injury in the course of writing *Achilles in Vietnam: Combat Trauma and the Undoing of Character.*[2]

Shay began work for the book in the early 1990s when rumors began to circulate about Vietnam veterans having been treated badly upon their return from the war. The stories spawned a "yellow ribbon" campaign during the Persian Gulf War that was used by pro-war conservatives to intimidate antiwar activists—opposition to the US commitment of troops to the Gulf was tantamount to Vietnam veterans having been spat on by protesters, according to the war's supporters. Despite being later debunked by historians, the stories of hostile homecomings from Vietnam provided putative evidence for a stabbed-in-the-back explanation for the loss of the war. Shay's affinity for those stories is nevertheless evinced in Chapter 1 of *Achilles in Vietnam* where he writes, "Much of the public treated [Vietnam veterans] with indifference or derision," words eponymic with the betrayal themes from Homer's *Iliad* that frame his book.[3]

In *Iliad*, writes Shay, Achilles has taken an enemy town, killed Briseis's husband and three brothers, and taken her as a trophy. When his commander Agamemnon claims Briseis for himself, Achilles feels violated, his sense of manly honor, as embodied in Briseis, had been stolen; that the wrongdoer was a trusted leader leaves Achilles feeling betrayed. Achilles's debasement by the man he looked up to is a moral injury, in Shay's interpretation, a hurt that manifests as a fit of violence later in the story.

Shay uses Achilles's story as an allegory for the betrayal experienced by Vietnam veterans upon return from their war. Not only was the military mission sold-out by weak-kneed politicians and campus agitators at home, but the respect normally accorded war veterans was denied to them; the populous that sent them off to fight, shunned them upon return.

Shay follows Homer's social-psychological tracks into the Vietnam's warzone, using veterans' stories of committing atrocities upon their leaders' orders, in opposition to their own sense of right and wrong. It was those infringements on their proprieties, the societal values they went to Vietnam with, that left them emotionally adrift when they returned. The personal disorientation of the war, coupled with the shock of home-front rejection, was a one-two gut-punch that was a blow to everything they believed in. With their moral bearings broken, Shay says, the Vietnam generation of veterans descended into the post-Vietnam syndrome later known as PTSD.

Moral Injury: Its Own Spectacle

The term moral injury was slow to gain traction with public and professional audiences. In the first 15 years after *Achilles's* 1994 publication, newspaper references to it averaged about three per year, a sign of merely incidental recognition. A PubMed search found zero entries for "moral injury" in 2010. The number climbed slowly until 2017 when it jumped to 21 from 12 the year before. In the next four years, it rose steadily to 159 in 2021.

Signaling his own premonitions that the book market might shrug at *Achilles*, Shay made a spectacle of his own work. On the page before the book's Introduction, he inserted the following:

CAUTION TO VETERAN'S, THEIR FAMILIES, AND THEIR FRIENDS
Please pace yourself and take care of yourself while reading even if it means stopping ad putting the book down. Some of the readings described here by your fellow veterans may trigger reactions in you that disrupt your life.

Shay's alarm bell rang for a full page. In legal circles, what he did would be called "leading the witness," a tactic disallowed in court; in literature, it's called "framing," a technique to predispose readers' acceptance of some information, and the dismissal of other. In his own profession, psychiatry, Shay's resort to "the power of suggestion" to elicit reader-patient buy-in to the "moral injury" paradigm his book was promoting would raise ethical issues.

More than one of his professional associates must have cringed at the sensationalism of Shay's warning to readers: a Freudian slip, of sorts, that gave away his self-doubt about what he had written? Nevertheless, the reaction to *Achilles* mixed praise with criticism. Pulitzer winner Robert Olen Butler's back-cover endorsement called it "brilliant on Greek classics" and the 1994 review in the prestigious *Virginia Quarterly Review* praised its creative use of Homer's poem for commentary on twentieth-century war.

The *VQR* reviewer, poet W.D. Ehrhart, also cited flaws in *Achilles*, including Shay's misreading of Homer and his misrepresentations of the war in Vietnam. About Shay's use of Agamemnon's abuse of Achilles as a war wound that spelled moral injury, Ehrhart points out that later, in Homer's Book 9, Agamemnon apologizes to Achilles and makes restitution for having hurt him. But Achilles refuses to accept the overtures, an act judged by Shay to be a moral failure and evidence of injury inflicted upon him by Agamemnon himself—moral injury. Ehrhart however, cites other studies suggesting that Achilles's own flawed character, brought with him to the war from earlier experience, was responsible for his ethical misstep with Agamemnon.

In fact, Ehrhart may have been more right than he knew in 1994. Historian Milton Bates's 1996 *The War's We Took to Vietnam* averred that the race, gender, and class conflicts of the 1950s and early 1960s shaped the social values and moral codes—the character traits—taken to Vietnam by US military personnel. By Bates's reckoning, the explanation that atrocities committed in Vietnam were due to the traumas experienced by G.I.s—Shay's "moral injury"—might be more accurately assigned to the growing-up experiences of young men in America. Bates's insight was supported by later clinical findings that veterans' family lives before military service was a better predictor of suicide than exposure to combat.

Achilles's text consists of long quotes from Homer's *Iliad* and numerous quotes from Vietnam veterans testifying to the combat trauma ostensibly responsible for the symptoms they presented. Shay was a psychiatrist working at the Boston Veterans Affairs Outpatient Clinic at the time, so he was undoubtedly seeing some troubled people. But Ehrhart said the doctor was all too willing to take at face value his patients' descriptions of their combat experiences.

Ehrhart, a Marine Corp veteran of heavy fighting at Hue in Vietnam during the 1968 Tet Offensive, singled out the claim made by one of Shay's patients that North Vietnamese troops, at the time, had "systematically hacked from [a hospital] patients' bodies any limbs they had found bandaged with American bandages and hooked up to American I.V.s."

In *Achilles*, Shay presented the story as an example of war-induced trauma that the veteran brought home.[4] But Ehrhart questions the validity of the story. "I have studied this battle and its aftermath at great length over the years since," he wrote "and I have never encountered such a story in any source, historical or literary, written or oral until now." Ehrhart then asked, "What are we to think about the veteran who has told this story, or about the author who reproduces it without question?"

Shay's *Achilles* is loaded with "war stories," exaggerations that enhance the combat credentials of the teller. "The stocks [of the M-16s] broke [in hand-to-hand combat]," reads Shay's quote of one veteran.[5] Hand-to-hand combat? In Vietnam? Maybe, in some obscure, one-off instance, but the broken M-16 stocks (note the plural) is the kind of story-telling prop that impugns the truth of the whole story. A dad hearing his young son exclaim, "Dad, dad, I caught a 15 lb. rainbow today!" is less likely to think the boy maybe caught a 3-pounder than nothing at all. The exaggeration intended to fill in the reality gap actually does the opposite, revealing the story-teller's embarrassment about the truth.

The tall tales riddling the war trauma literature are understandable as strategies for attaining VA benefits or sympathy from friends and family. Chapter 3 described the phenomenon known as "factitious PTSD" involving veterans who report PTSD-like symptoms to clinicians and inflate their wartime experience to bolster their claim. And the problem isn't limited to Vietnam veterans. In a September 2021 *New York Times* story, "For Veterans, The Trauma Doesn't End with Service," a veteran claimed to have been hospitalized for PTSD, and to being 90% disabled. He said he had been in the Army infantry for 8 years with two deployments to Iraq and one to Afghanistan and made the untenable boast: "There wasn't a day went by that I did not fire my weapon in combat."[6]

The claim to have PTSD is also found in legal defense cases as an alibi for homicide. Massachusetts' Governor William Weld pardoned Joseph Yandle, convicted in 1992 for second degree murder, after hearing Yandle's claim that trauma suffered in Vietnam accounted for his crime. Yandle's case could have been cited by Shay—if he had not been *re*arrested after it was found that he had never been in Vietnam. In January 2008, the *New York Times* began a series about 121 veterans of the wars in Iraq and Afghanistan who had been charged with homicide for killings committed after their return from service abroad. About a third of the victims were spouses, girlfriends, and children. Some the cases in the series are remindful of those described as "berserkers" in Shay's *Achilles*, and some strain the credibility of the connections made by the *Times* journalists between the service records of those accused, the crimes committed, and the alibis constructed by their lawyers.[7]

Seen Combat? Who's to Say?

Shay's method itself raises the most serious questions about the validity of *Achilles*. Who is he talking about? Discerning readers would notice the modifier "combat" attached to every use of "veteran" that he associates with moral injury. In other words, his claims that this or that percentage of Vietnam veterans suffer moral injury is limited to *combat* veterans. If 100 out of 1,000 Vietnam veterans present the symptoms of moral injury, he could claim a 10% rate of injury. But if only *combat* veterans are counted, maybe the ratio changes to 100 out of 300, a 30% injury rate—a more eye-catching figure. The question then becomes how "combat" is defined.

In fact, there are no official designations for "combat" or "combat veterans." There is the old term, "combat arms," that referred to the infantry, armor, and artillery branches of the army. But that classification elevated the cooks and clerk-typists of an artillery battery to the same combat status as its 155-M gun crews; not very accurate—unless you were a cook on Firebase Schueller in Vietnam's Central Highlands the night it was overrun.

The Combat Infantry Badge (CIB) is a more precise standard for combat status. A CIB recipient "must be personally present and under hostile fire while serving in an assigned infantry or Special Forces primary duty, in a unit actively engaged in ground combat with the enemy ..."[8] But the terms for a CIB award are subject to definition and interpretation: What does "primary duty" mean? Actively engaged"? "Ground combat"? And what about the judgment of the officer or non-commissioned officer (NCO) recommending the award—any room for biases and prejudices at play there?

Another standard is the Combat Index created in 1981 by the Center for Policy Research for the Veterans Administration. The Index listed 12 items, each weighted by their frequency of occurrence: rarely, sometimes, often, or very often. A veteran had to score at least 2.99 total points to qualify as a "combat" veteran. Item #4 read, "received incoming fire." But what did "incoming fire" mean? I was in Vietnam in 1969. A mortar round landing on my guard bunker would count as "incoming fire." If it landed 10 feet away, it would still count, right? But what about a barrage of multiple rounds landing 50 feet or 50 yards away? Who's to say? Who at the VA could judge my description of events to say if I did or did not meet the standard for combat-veteran status?

Shay says that 35.8% of *combat* veterans met the diagnostic criteria for PTSD in the late 1980s.[9] He might have been right but it's hard to square that number with the widely accepted figure that only about 15% of the military personnel in Vietnam saw combat, or with psychiatrist Peter Bourne's 1973 report (see Chapter 3) that psychiatric casualties were more common among rear echelon non-combatants than combat troops.

Definitions of combat bedeviled the discourse on war trauma well into the conflicts in Iraq and Afghanistan. In an August 2011 article, *New York Times* reporter Benedict Carey, citing a new article in *Journal of the American Medical Association* about the use of an Antipsychotic drug, Risperdal, to treat PTSD wrote that, "Up to 20 percent of those who see heavy combat have lasting signs of post-traumatic stress disorder." Skeptical of categories like "heavy combat," and knowing the powerful subtexts they carry, I searched the news story for how it was defined—but found nothing. Looking at the *JAMA* article cited by the reporter, I saw that the researchers had used no such category. I asked a doctor at a Veterans Administration hospital how and why the reporter might have come up with the term, and she said, "I don't know—he made it up."[10]

On one level, the reporter's invention of "heavy combat" for his story might seem to be of little consequence since he seemed to have reported the rest of the *JAMA* article accurately. On another level, though, it clouds the interpretation of the data: if at most 20% of *heavy-combat* veterans have PTSD, that could reduce the number of plausibly traumatized veterans-of-all-levels considerably—depending, again, on how the term is defined. The more likely (and serious) fallout from what the reporter wrote, however, was another instance of "combat" and PTSD being used circularly to credential each other. In the context of two decades of PTSD and combat being woven through popular, medical, and political culture, it's as likely as not that the association between PTSD and "heavy combat" in the story registers with the casual reader as, "all veterans with PTSD saw heavy combat." In fact, the journal article's intent was to say, "some veterans who saw heavy combat will have PTSD."

What Did *You* Do in the War, Daddy?

Shay's incessant reminder to readers that it is *combat* veterans that he is talking about is conspicuous, making us wonder if it is more for sound-effect than analytic rigor. Like the bull-horned CAUTION TO VETERANS that he led with, it seems like a pitch to the American fascination with combat and the men associated with it.

On August 17, 2009, President Barack Obama spoke to the Veterans of Foreign Wars (VFW) convention in Phoenix, Arizona. For two consecutive hours in mid-day, newscasters for National Public Radio reported that the president was speaking before an organization of "combat" veterans. A casual identification of the VFW with combat veterans would be understandable. After all, service abroad in the US military for the last 100 years has often involved wars on foreign soil. But not all foreign service, even in war zones, involves combat. In fact, the VFW is open to all veterans who have served abroad. What's interesting, then, is what it is that presses the term "combat" into inappropriate usage, even by the carefully edited NPR newscasters—even by Dr. Shay.[11]

Calling the VFW an organization of "combat" veterans is a way of saying its members are *special*, a cut above ordinary veterans. Combat experience is a credential for authority on social and political issues. Dwight D. Eisenhower oversaw the 1942 invasion of Normandy, France and on the basis of that, won the Presidency in 1952. John F. Kennedy's heroism in the Second World War also took him to the White House. Several veterans of Vietnam including Senators John McCann, John Kerry, and Jim Webb bounced off their records in combat for successful political careers. The President's stature is raised by his appearance before this august gathering.[12]

In Western culture, military duty is the rite of passage from boyhood to manhood. The temptation for men to exaggerate their records in combat is understandably greatest for veterans whose actual performance in war does not live up to what they think the society expects of them. Sometimes those expectations, having been formed by Hollywood film or other fictional sources, are unrealistic inventions intended to entertain rather than inform. In Vietnam, for example, a GI with his helmet unbuckled, cigarette dangling from his lip, and a bandolier of ammunition draped around his neck might pose for a photograph knowing that the pose would interest the folks back home."[13]

The problem of unrealistic expectations put on male veterans has grown over recent decades. Bombing runs over North Vietnam in the 1960s and 1970s often originated in Thailand or the Philippines where pilots and crews lived in air-conditioned quarters with amenities like swimming pools and libraries located well beyond the range of enemy retaliation. Sometimes, the flyers knew nothing more about their targets than the coordinates for the bomb drop—and even less about the people they were killing.[14]

Twenty-first-century war has become automated to a point where the soldier has been reduced, in some cases, to a joy-stick appendage delivering remote-controlled weaponry to targets miles away. In March 2009 reports surfaced of drones operated from Arizona being deployed against suspected al Qaeda targets in Pakistan: the operators went home to their families for evening dinner. That's an extreme example of war so automated as to deprive the men involved of any meaningful sense of soldierly accomplishment, but it's really just an extension of trends underway for most of the last century.[15]

False claims to battlefront valor led to the passage in 2006 of the Stolen Valor Act that made it a federal crime to lie about being a military hero. Thousands of cases are reported each year according to Doug Sterner who tracks down the phonies, and 60 have been prosecuted under the Act that he helped draft.[16]

Atrocities and Moral Injury: A Troublesome Mix

The reach for combat identity has tangled meanings of "combat" and "war trauma" such that combat experience and trauma diagnoses validate one another: a veteran's combat bona fides qualify him for a trauma diagnosis; a trauma diagnosis credentials his standing as a combat veteran. It's a knot that tightens when veteran claims to have committed an atrocity come into the picture.

In his book *War Stories*, historian Gary Kulik has a chapter entitled "False Atrocities" filled with stories about G.I.s and marines killing unarmed Vietnamese or opposing forces so inadequately provisioned that their killing would have constituted war crimes—if they were true. But the stories are loaded with exaggeration, some of them preposterous and unbelievable. He begins the chapter with a vignette about "Turk." Turk tells of being a tunnel rat for the 1st Infantry Division in the Iron Triangle north of Saigon. On one mission to ferret Viet Cong from their underground lair, he goes deeply into the tunnel complex and then risks his own life, pulling the pins on several hand grenades by his teeth and tossing them into a hole where he is sure there are enemy soldiers. Reluctant to finish the story about his heroic action (which listeners are certain must have earned him a medal), Turk eventually responds to a request: no medal, he explained, "I blew up a teacher with a classroom full of kids."[17]

Kulik, the author, then reveals to us that Turk was "a wannabe vet" who had never been in Vietnam. Kulik's chapter is full of phony atrocity stories like Turk's, and he puzzles over why historians and reporters so often buy into them when details like pulling grenade pins with teeth happen only in screenwriters' imaginations.

Shay's *Achilles* is full of atrocity stories ostensibly told to him by his patients. One that he tells on page 1 of Chapter 1, and repeats later in the book, tells of a Long Range Patrol (LURP) team seeing weapons being unloaded at night from boats along the shore of the South China Sea. When the LURP team got positioned on the boats, his patient tells him,

> We opened up on them—aah. And the fucking firepower was unreal, the firepower that we put into them boats. It was constant ... It seemed like no one ever ran out of ammo. Daylight came [long pause], and we found out we killed a lot of fishermen and kids.

The LURP veteran, says Shays, was awarded the CIB for the action and now feels "deeply dishonored" by the award, a tragic victim suffering the moral injury of the atrocity he committed.

This could be the tale of two tales, but the difference in the way Kulik and Shay use their stories is significant. Kulik uses his to illustrate the lengths to which men sometimes go to ID themselves as real deal, hardcore, combat veterans, and how post-Vietnam War American culture facilitated that sort of exercise. And Kulik does this by debunking the truth of the story. Shay, on the other hand, does not engage his storyteller at all. It might be that the LURP veteran's story is legit but, given the centrality of the story to his book, it is more than surprising that he did not interrogate its validity, nor any of the other scores of stories like it that he heard from patients.

The Consequences of "Moral Injury"

Shay's determination to establish a collective portrait of Vietnam veterans as victims of the war they fought has consequences. One is that he writes out the counter-narrative that for thousands of G.I.s, marines, airmen, and sailors the war was a consciousness raising experience. Certainly, American troops committed disgraceful acts, a fact documented in Nick Turse's book, *Kill Anything That Moves*. But they also displayed courageous acts of compassion like Warrant Officer Hugh Thompson's who intervened to save lives at My Lai in 1968; there were the troops of the Americal Division that refused to go on patrol in solidarity with the stateside Moratorium Days against the war in 1969; there were the prisoners of war (POWs) held in Hanoi who voiced their opposition to the war under threat of court-martial upon their release; there was Green Beret Sergeant Donald Duncan who deployed to Vietnam in 1964 and "quit" the army in protest of the war after seeing intelligence reports showing it to be "a lie."[18]

Shay takes a pass on the chance to pursue the storyline of war resistance within the US military even when it appears in his own material. He tells us that "fragging" was "a widely acknowledged impulse" among combat troops in Vietnam and describes it as "slang for assassination of one's military superior." But he embeds this short entrée under the chapter subheads, "deprivation" and "friendly fire," and uses a scene from Homer to discern the meaning of fragging.

When Achilles draws his sword against Agamemnon to avenge his betrayal, goddess Athena stops him. By Shay's interpretation, Agamemnon's slaying, his fragging, would have been a "deprivation" suffered by Agamemmon. Transferred to the war in Vietnam, the tale casts the fragged officers as casualties of "friendly fire," their assailants as misguided victims of moral injury, not warriors against the war.[19]

Just as PTSD, Agent Orange, and TBI function to displace political veterans from the American story, so too does Shay's moral injury—only more thoroughly. The other three terms, and PTSD especially, engage with the antiwar discourse brought to the conversation by veterans. But *Achilles* drops them out of the record altogether; there are no antiwar G.I.s or veterans in this 246-page book. None. Zero. Period.

Shay's dismissal of politicized troops is ironic because it conflicts with the notion of "communialization of trauma" that he puts forward as the best treatment for moral injury. Communialization appears to be a coinage of Shay's that he leaves undefined. However, the term itself and his suggestion that treatment of moral injury must be "social" call forth sociological considerations of his patients' plights; his catchphrase, "healing is done *by* survivors, not *to* survivors" (his italics), presumably puts patients' peers on the front line of his strategy—but we don't see them in *Achilles*'s pages on war trauma healing and therapy.[20]

Most men returned to their families, workplaces, and schools when they returned from Vietnam. Some experienced adjustment problems like returnees from other wars. Some were hospitalized with wounds that included the psychiatric casualties that Peter Bourne wrote about in 1973. Among the "survivors" of moral injury that Shay referred to were more than 20,000 antiwar veterans who integrated with the social movements opposed to the war; some, helped set up storefront counseling centers for their peers having difficulty reentering civilian life. The very troops that Shay elides from his story, in other words, the men politicized and empowered by their experience at war and having returned *without* moral injury, and asymptomatic of war trauma, were the communalizing agents that remain off screen in his account—for they, too, in his view are damaged goods unqualified to show others the way home.

The spectacle of a whole generation of morally injured veterans was catnip for the press and medical establishment as a new generation of soldiers boarded planes for wars in the Middle East. Moral injury, the phrase, crept up from one newspaper entry in 2001 to nine in 2010 before jumping to 21 in 2011 and 89 in 2015. Per the pattern of professional interest in new diagnoses—see previous chapters—its rise in the medical literature lagged that in newspapers, but by 2021 it was on the minds of mental health providers and in the pages of their journals.

The embrace of the moral injury perspective by liberals such as the Lynds undermined the credibility of Vietnam veterans as a voice within the antiwar movement. In *Moral Injury and Nonviolent Resistance,* they write that moral injury "caused many soldiers in the U.S. Army to stop fighting in the early 1970s." But that is an imposition of Shay's thinking that inverts the more likely logic that those troops refused orders precisely because they were *not* morally compromised. While resisters' senses of right and wrong were always in play, class-based resentments of military authority and the anti-imperialist politics of the stateside antiwar movement were almost certainly a greater influence.

Shay's influence, through writers like the Lynds, reproduces the political or psychological dichotomy in how the dissident-veteran behavior is viewed. The choice has consequences for the way the Vietnam generation of veterans is seen by its successors. A film such as the 2006 *Sir! No Sir!* presented in-service resistors as role models for battling the brass, and veterans as counter-hegemonic figures and voices in a deepening twenty-first-century militarist culture. The 2017 PBS documentary *The Vietnam War*, on the other hand, portrays Vietnam veterans most prominently as victims of not only the war but the antiwar movement upon their return home.

Moral Injury a Dog Whistle for MAGA

Betrayal. Betrayal is the bedrock of moral injury. Agamemnon in *Iliad* is a leader, an authority figure. His position as commander entails commitments to his men, obligations that set their expectations of what they can ask of and receive from him. It is the violation of those expectations, their betrayal that lies at the core of *Achilles*, as Shay reads it.

Transferred to post-Vietnam War America, *Achilles* cues the perception that the war had been lost because the political and military authorities had failed to meet soldiers' expectations that they would have the material and leadership necessary to win the war. The establishment had failed them, and worse, the political left had given aid and comfort to the enemy and sapped their fighting spirit. "The returning Vietnam soldiers were not honored," Shay writes in *Achilles*. "Much of the public treated them with indifference or derision ..." Six years later, after the myth of hostile homecomings had been debunked, he repeated the right-wing canard that "veterans returned home to protesters who accused them of being torturers, perpetrators of atrocities, and baby killers."[21]

Moral injury, the concept, entered the mainstream war trauma vocabulary at the time when the search for biomarkers that would validate PTSD and the diagnoses spun from it were showing little promise. Veteran advocates, journalists, and mental health columnists were looking for a way out of the dead end at which war trauma studies had arrived—even if that path led away from scientific discourse.

The notion of moral injury has no materiality, no empirical tangency—what, after all, is injured when a "moral" is injured? It is Greek *myth* that leads the thinking, not observation or logic, the substance of science. Whereas a writer like H. Bruce Franklin uses "myth" in his *M.I.A. or Mythmaking in America*, to *describe* claims that US POWs were held by communists in Vietnam long after the war ended, Shay uses myth as a validating quality of moral injury, as if its mythical DNA certifies its realness.

Moral injury is an ethereal something-or-other, an empty vessel that can be filled with whatever by whomever. Shay fills it with pacifist feelings. His desires for peace, healing, and the recovery of his patients are admirable. But moral injury's conceptual vacuity makes it useful for the same nefarious forces that arose in interwar Europe to whip victim-veteran sentiments into a fascist front.

The resort to nonrational discourse in the war trauma literature is part and parcel of the resurgent traditionalism that is fueling religious fundamentalism and authoritarian politics around the world. In the United States that trend manifests as skepticism of medical science, an embrace of traditional family values, identity politics, and return to a mythical America of yesteryear.

Notes

1 Jan Barry is a founder of Vietnam veterans of America and an acclaimed antiwar poet. Bill Ehrhart, featured in the 2017 PBS film *The Vietnam War*, taught at the Haverford School, and is said to be the "Dean of Vietnam War Poetry." Charlie Clements graduated second in his class at the Air Force Academy and flew missions in Vietnam before citing moral grounds for refusing to fly more; he later became a doctor and won an Academy Award for his film 1986 film *Witness to War* documenting resistance to US client regime in El Salvador. Chuck Searcy returned to Vietnam in 1992 to help find and defuse unexploded bombs (A Lingering, Deadly Legacy of Wars: Unexploded Bombs—*The New York Times* (nytimes.com).

2 Lynd and Lynd, *Moral Injury and Nonviolent Resistance*, 1.

3 Shay, *Achilles*, 7.

4 Ibid., 104.

5 Ibid., 158.

6 Steinhauer, "For Veterans, the Trauma Doesn't End with Service."

7 There is more about the *Times* series in Lembcke, *PTSD: Diagnosis and Identity in Post-Empire America*.

8 See Combat Infantryman Badge—Wikipedia.

9 Shay, *Achilles*, 168.

10 I messaged the reporter, Benedict Carey, on August 28, 2011, to ask if he had some other source for the "heavy combat" designation but I have not heard back.

11 At vfw.org and the link to "Am I eligible?" one finds the criteria for membership in Veterans of Foreign Wars, some of which entail having a "campaign medal" for service in a military unit assigned to a place for a certain operation. A clerk typist assigned to a headquarters unit in Vietnam, and not normally exposed to combat, would qualify for membership, as well as an infantry rifleman. A campaign medal for "Operation Uphold Democracy" in Haiti, September 16, 1994 to March 31, 1995, entitles the holder to membership. (One US soldier was killed during the operation.) A two-day Vietnam "campaign" called "Frequent Wind" April 29–30, 1975 earns eligibility for the holder.

12 Shephard, *War of Nerves,* 18, recalls the words of military historian Sir Michael Howard about Edwardian England: "For the best part of a hundred years, war did indeed 'define masculinity' in British society. War was a test of Manhood."

13 Urbina, "In Ranks of Heroes, Find the Fakes," reports the problem of false military identities and disability claims: "in April 2009 the Department of Veterans Affairs was paying disability benefits to 286 supposed prisoners of war from the Persian Gulf War ... and to 966 supposed prisoners of the Vietnam War. But Defense Department

records show that only 21 prisoners of war returned from the Gulf War, and that fewer than 600 are alive from the Vietnam War." Urbina goes on to write that, "tales of physical or psychological suffering can influence whether a veteran receives some money or nothing at all in disability payments …"

14 The memoirs written by the pilots shot down over North Vietnam and held as POWs in Hanoi contain numerous references to the upscale living conditions they enjoyed before making their last and fateful bombing runs (Wilber and Lembcke, *Dissenting POWs*). Lair, *Armed with Abundance*, 76–86, writes that conditions for G.I.s even within Vietnam were often as good as stateside. To provide fresh dairy products including ice cream, the military contracted the operation of several dairy plants located throughout the South.

15 Zulaika, *Hellfire from Paradise Ranch: On the Frontlines of Drone Warfare.*

16 Frosch, "Fighting for the Right to Tell Lies."

17 Kulik, *War Stories: False Atrocity Stories*, 181 reconstructs Turk's story-telling from Samuel Haynes's book *The Soldiers' Tale.*

18 The cover of the February 1966 antiwar publication *Ramparts* was a photograph of the gritty, square-jawed Duncan in uniform beneath the large block letters: "I Quit."

19 Shay, *Achilles*, 21–27.

20 Ibid., 187.

21 Ibid., 7; Shay, "The Betrayal of 'What's Right'," 82.

7

TRAUMA IN A POST-TRUTH ERA

Back to Charcot's Salon?

The idea of war trauma is an imperious force. In the American post-Vietnam War era, traumatized war veterans became the metamorphic stand-ins for the nation's loss of pride and superiority. Knocked off its self-imagined perch as City on the Hill, the country went into the twenty-first century confused and anxious about its future, an identity crisis that seeped into its popular and political cultures. Novelists and screenwriters plying the trauma narrative—even reinterpreting historical work through the trauma lens, as is shown in this chapter—and political figures eager to exploit unsettled emotions for personal gain, fueled a back-to-the-future revanchism with existential implications.

The embrace of moral injury as a way to think and write about war trauma took its enthusiasts beyond the fact-based world into the realm of mental health phantasmagoria. Its definitional blankness cast aspersions on the scientific integrity of its conceptual forebearer, post-traumatic stress disorder (PTSD), confirming along the way the value of the war-trauma lexicon as a cultural discourse.

The result, captured by Parul Sehgal for the December 2021 *New Yorker Magazine*, is that trauma has become an "all-engulfing" trope. Filmmakers can't resist it, she said, and fiction writers love it. The 636,120 "symptom combinations" now attributable to PTSD Sehgal wrote, makes it the fourth most common diagnosis for psychiatric disorders in America. With a nod to Jonathon Shay, she notes the fusion of medical and moral meanings in PTSD that allows war veterans having committed atrocities to "share" the trauma of their victims and spouses and children of veterans to claim their father's trauma.[1]

James Robins used the notion of "vicarious trauma" for his February 16, 2021, article in the *New Republic*, "Can Historians Be Traumatized by History." Vicarious traumatization involves imagination and empathy, he wrote. It is impossible for historians to document the past without "re-creating the ambience

DOI: 10.4324/9781003391906-8

of other lives" and entering their experience, he said. And "the more fervent, precise, or visionary their reconstructions of the past, and the more completely they immerse themselves, the more harshly they may be wounded by what they study."[2]

Historians "wounded" by the subjects they write about might be better suited for coffee room talk than the therapist's couch, but its flipside is less prosaic: historians imbued with trauma-centric paradigms reinterpreting existing historical literature to fit the currently popular trauma narratives. A case in point is Tom Roston's 2021 reread of Kurt Vonnegut's antiwar classic *Slaughterhouse Five* through the lens of the trauma plot.[3] Vonnegut created Billy Pilgrim as a character in his 1973 novel and used Billy as an avatar through which he tells his own story of being a POW in the Second World War. Held by Germans in an animal slaughterhouse in Dresden, Germany he had seen terrible things which are remembered by Billy after the war.

Billy Pilgrim Psychologized

Written over several years during the war in Vietnam, *Slaughterhouse Five* has been read and applauded by critics as one of the great antiwar novels of the twentieth century. Billy's flights of fancy and nightmares mixed war imagery with scary experiences he had before and after the war. Remembering his flight from German pursuers in the Battle of the Bulge, for example, he stops in the forest: "Leaning against a tree, his head tilted back and his nostrils flaring," Billy remembered his father teaching him to swim by the "sink-or-swim" method. His father was "going to throw Billy into the deep end, and Billy was going to damn well swim. It was like an execution … When he opened his eyes, he was at the bottom of the pool and there was beautiful music everywhere."[4] In that fusion of Billy's remembered childhood experience with his real-time experience running from German captors, Vonnegut shows us how mistaken it would be to reduce Billy's later memory of the war to that moment in the forest.

I read *Slaughterhouse Five* in the early 1970s after return from Vietnam and have always thought of it as a great commentary on the awfulness of war. Vonnegut, a WWII veteran was using his war and post-war experience to validate what I and other Vietnam veterans were feeling. Rereading it 50 years later, the surreality of the memory-dream-escapism synthesis created by Vonnegut, through Billy, still seems authentic.

But the historian-critic Roston is immersed in the literary trauma-cult that Sehgal describes. Jonathon Shay figures prominently in his revisit of *Slaughterhouse Five*; Karl Marlantes who regaled viewers of Ken Burns and Lynn Novick's 2017 *The Vietnam War* with tales of protesters' attacks on veterans, blurbs the book. While Vonnegut gives us reasons to think that Billy Pilgrim might have been bipolar and depressed even if he had never been in the war, Roston is not having it. Iraq War veteran and writer Matthew Mellina told Roston, "I feel Vonnegut wanted to give personification to PTSD. And Billy Pilgrim was his way,"[5] In other words, we have good reason to think that it is *Rolston*'s makeover of Vonnegut's character that gives us a PTSD-stricken Billy Pilgrim, not Vonnegut himself.

Billy Pilgrim's Creator Psychologized

And doesn't Roston do the same with *his* subject, Kurt Vonnegut? He quotes Vonnegut saying, "The importance of Dresden in my life has been considerably exaggerated," and quotes Vonnegut's denial that "trauma could apply to him." Roston nevertheless insists that Vonnegut wrote *Slaughterhouse Five* as catharsis for his war experience. In support of his pathologized Vonnegut, Roston cites unpublished archival material where the novelist wrote, "I suppose that I was slightly crazy when I got home from that war." Uncontextualized as Roston leaves it, the "crazy" could be just a figure of speech.[6]

Roston also digs up pre- and post-war details about Vonnegut's life that can explain why he created the auto-biographical Billy: his childhood home was "filled with tension between parents who had raging arguments"; his mother was manic depressive and addicted to barbiturates; she committed suicide on the eve of his departure to the war; his father's early death in 1957 put him "into a creative spiral"; two years later, his sister's husband died in a train accident just days before she died of cancer.[7]

In later years, Vonnegut drank too much, he was depressed, seeing a psychiatrist, and contemplating suicide. His son, Mark, had a "schizophrenic break" in 1971, which coupled with his mother's mental illness, establishes a family line of disorders along which Vonnegut's own problems can be understood—without reference to the war, if one wants to. Roston did not.

Trauma as Spectacle

Kurt Vonnegut was a hero-writer. Reducing him to a war casualty seeking redemption and healing through his writing—which is what Roston does—displaces the political content and consequences of *Slaughterhouse Five*. In the same manner that PTSD created a victim-veteran image that competed with the politicized persona that many Vietnam veterans brought home from the war, it is used in *The Writer's Crusade* as a way to psychologize Vonnegut.

Roston's psychologically wounded war veteran, Vonnegut, is *his* creation, a figure evocative of the victims of fascist violence in Italy that the fascists themselves then used as spectacles, props to generate the emotional excitation that could be manipulated for their nefarious purposes. Roston does not exploit his Vonnegut in this way, but he constructs his character out of materials meant to do that and which have been put that use by others: PTSD was used to demean the political character of antiwar Vietnam veterans, and cobble the home front betrayal narrative for the loss of the war; the herbicide Agent Orange was made over to a mental health idiom; "trauma" was appended to "brain injury," aka concussion, to sensationalize the effects of improvised explosive devices in Iraq; moral injury made war casualties a quasi-religious consideration, a discourse with spiritual tones attractive to the liberal faith community.

As the linage of war-trauma terminology lengthened, its quality became more inventive, a trend in keeping with a societal shift away from empirical science as a basis for truth to more traditional bases found in emotion, imagination, and intuition.

Forward: From Modern Rationality to Pre-modernism Spectacle

In a June 30, 2022, *New York Times* letter to the editor, psychologist Robert Silverstone contended that Donald Trump's persistence in claiming he won the 2020 presidential election means he is either lying or delusional, the latter a mental illness, Silverstone points out. "Which is it?" he ends by asking.

But those choices are framed by modernist epistemologies, ways of knowing that value empirical measures of truth and rationality. What if we step out of that box and ask not whether large numbers of people act on information they think is true, but on information that touches their feelings? What if they are more likely to follow leaders who stir their passions and excite their hopes than leaders whose speech and mannerisms sound learned and appear authoritative? What if, in other words, to ask if Donald Trump is lying or telling the truth, if he is sane or not, is to ask the wrong questions because the *lingua franca* of American politics has become *spectacle*.

Donald Trump traffics in spectacle. When he claimed that his January 20, 2021, inauguration day parade drew "a million, million and a half" supporters, an Associated Press fact check disputed the numbers. Liberal critics said his claim was a lie. But the liar charge missed the point: Trump could wear it as a badge of honor, a raised finger to mainstream media's fixation with numbers as documentable "facts" vs. the narrative that he was now the President loved by many. The truth of the matter-for-the-day was in what people along the parade route *believed* it to be, not in what the evidence on the ground said it was. In the adjudication of the powers of persuasion, spectacle had won out over data.

Trump's penchant for spectacle had been on display for years in his reality TV show, "The Apprentice," his appetite for the grandiosity of luxury hotels and casinos, and his showy, orange-tinted hair, for which rapper Busta Rhymes dubbed him, "Agent Orange." When he stalked the Democratic Party presidential candidate Hillary Clinton on stage during the televised debates for the 2016 election, pacing behind her as she spoke, many viewers were outraged, certain that such loutish behavior would cost him the election. His supporters were just as certain that his flaunt of the debates' staging, with its practiced exchanges between candidates, had channeled widespread disgust with political curation—and that they, the voters, would see Trump as having exposed electoral democracy as a meaningless ritual.[8]

Liberal critics saw what Trump did as an attempt to intimidate Clinton—she was the target. But communication theory rooted in the Frankfort School studies of twentieth-century European fascism would suggest that his real target was the television audience, his actions a spectacle that said, louder than words, that people could be moved by what they saw and felt, more than by what they were asked to think about.

Trump's televised upstaging of Clinton was a dramatic violation of American political etiquette, but it resurfaced as a snub of medical science in 2020. On January 29, the White House established a coronavirus taskforce to deal with the spread of Covid-19; Dr. Anthony Fauci, Director of the National Institute of Allergy and Diseases was appointed to lead the taskforce. On February 10 Trump said the virus would be gone by April, but offered "no scientific information to support that," according to *USA Today*. A week later, the paper quoted Dr. Fauci saying "it would be a stretch to assume it's going to disappear with warm weather."[9]

The Trump–Fauci relationship would not stay on a give-and-take terrain. In mid-March, the President declared the anti-malarial drug hydroxychloroquine to be a "game changer" in the treatment of Covid-19. When Dr. Fauci replied at a March 20 press conference that the President's claim for hydroxychloroquine was based on "anecdotal evidence," Trump stepped in front of the microphone, cutting him off and signaling to viewers that anecdotal evidence was good enough if the truth it told was the truth they wanted—it was a Clinton debate moment, *redux*.

The truth in question at the hydroxychloroquine moment was less about the drug's effectiveness in fighting Covid-19 than its discursive value in the rising skepticism about modern science. While the efficacy of *medical* science was on the docket of the moment, its interlocutors had company among environmental activists and food-nutrition researchers, among others, who were stepping back from the cutting edges of science in their fields, and reconnecting with the wisened ways of traditional societies: some rivers, damned and channeled on the advice of engineers, were being returned to wetlands; lab-made fertilizers and pesticides better for agribusiness than human consumption were being swapped out for locavore diets and biologically diverse farming practices. For that matter, holistic health treatments found in Indigenous cultures were competing with Big Pharma market shares.

The tension between Trump and his science advisors tightened in the weeks leading to the November 2020 election. Speaking at an October 18 campaign rally, Trump mocked Democratic Party candidate Joe Biden for saying he, Biden, would "listen to the scientists." The next day, CNN reported Trump saying that "people are tired of hearing about the deadly pandemic" [and] trashed Dr. Anthony Fauci as a "disaster" who has been around for "500 years." He "referred to Fauci and other health officials as 'idiots'," according to CNN.[10]

Trump's bid for an audience was offensive, a demonstration of his ignorance about the standards of science and contempt for presidential decorum. It's possible, of course, that his insults were performative, displays of communicative genius in a league with the best of the twentieth-century's demagogues. But there is little in his background to suggest that he was familiar enough with that history, much less its political and philosophical meaning, to be very purposeful in what he was doing. Trump, however, was not flying solo, and his backseater, Steve Bannon, knew where they were going.

Steve Bannon: The White House Whisperer

Bannon was the CEO of the 2016 Trump campaign. He and Trump had been brought together by the billionaire hedge fund manager Robert Mercer and his daughter Rebekah, a philanthropist and major funder of the Goldwater Institute, a think tank, and the Heritage Foundation. They were financial backers of Breitbart News that Bannon became head of in 2012. In 2013, Rebekah and Bannon started Reclaim New York, a conservative watchdog operation, to monitor government spending. With Mercer money in 2014, Bannon created Cambridge Analytica, a data-mining company adept at the oppositional research that played a central role in the 2016 presidential campaign.

In his 2020 book *War for Eternity: Inside Bannon's Far-Right Circle of Global Power Brokers*, anthropologist Benjamin Teitelbaum describes Bannon as a "bookworm" with ties to a coterie of world leaders networked by belief in *Traditionalism*. Traditionalism, with the capital T, is a centuries-old philosophical and spiritual school of thought inspiring an obscure and underground movement that is now surfacing in real-world politics. Traditionalists, according to Teitelbaum, are anti-capitalist, anti-corporate, opposed to commercial cultural, and adamantly anti-globalist. Bannon's assertion, in the author's words, "that the working class is the fount of authenticity in inauthentic modern society" echoes the thinking of Western postmodern theorists that modernism is best at covering-over the reality of class relations in capitalism and creating illusions of stability and progress; those oppressed by the system, workers and peasants, are best able to see through its facades, according to the theory.[11]

Traditionalists, and acolytes such as Trump, pander to rural and nativist populations that are all too ready to flip-off intellectual elites with their highfalutin academic degrees. It is a small circle of power brokers that includes Aleksandr Dugin, an advisor to Vladimir Putin in Russia, Gabor Vona who has the ear of Hungary's Prime Minister Viktor Orban, and Olavo Carvalho in Brazil, said by Bannon to be the "great theorist" of then President Eduardo Bolsonaro's government.

Traditionalists believe that humankind was ushered into *darkness* by the European age of En*light*enment. It was the displacement of the symbolic and emotional by the rational, literal, quantifiable in the seventeenth and eighteenth centuries that separated the spiritualism of antiquity from the rationality and materialism of modernity; the crass consumerism of modern society that reduced relationships between people to the invidious comparisons of their possessions. Existence, in their belief, is cyclical, a notion that abjures progress, a staple of

Enlightenment thought. They are profoundly anti-modern which means they are disdainful of science. Loyalty, on the other hand, is a premodern virtue. It is no surprise, then, that when loyalty to the President conflicted with the data-driven policy choices made by White House scientists, the latter were brushed off and Republican rightists rallied to Trump.

The religious fundamentalism latent in Trump's back-to-the-future rhetoric is music to the ears of Americans feeling left behind by modernism, the calls to "tear it all down" raised by the end-of-timers among the Traditionalists a dangerous incitement in a world with the nuclear arms and chemical pathogens to do just that.

MAGA's Call: A New Zion or Nihilism?

Prelapsarian beliefs, betrayal, and apocalypticism are powerful themes in Christian fundamentalism. The vision of an idyllic Garden of Eden that preexisted mankind's fall into sin came with the promise that reconciliation with God would bring believers to eternity in a new Promised Land. Along the way, they would be lured by false gods offering here-and-now relief from their worldly miseries—they would be betrayed, for their sufferings were God's tests of their faith in Him alone as their Savior. At the end of time, only those who had rejected the temptations of earthly solutions would be raptured, saved from a fiery apocalypse for a heavenly reconciliation with their Creator.

Visions of the apocalypse are elemental to the fundamentalists' readings of the Bible's Book of Revelation. From time to time, throughout the colonial period and the early years of the nation, they manifested in periods of rapid social change and religious revivalism that sometimes spawned fears of betrayal by enemy aliens masquerading as patriots. After the McCarthyite hysteria of the 1950s, however, those religious undertones faded into the backstory of America's political history.

Americans growing up in the late 1950s and early 1960s would have heard the word "apocalypse" only in a religion-education class, if at all. The 1921 silent film *Four Horsemen of the Apocalypse* was remade for a 1962 release, but it had little to do with religion or politics. The *New York Times* uses of the word in any context between 1955 and 1965 numbered exactly zero. Between 1965 and 1975 it appeared in 21 stories but then increased in use over the next ten years to 369. The American fascination with the end-of-time had begun.[12]

One need look no further than the titles of twentieth-first-century movies and books to see the extent of apocalyptic themes in American popular culture. One search of film titles returned over 900 such references, including *Apocalypse 2012: The World after Time Ends*, *Apocalypse: World War II*, and *Zombie Apocalypse 2012*, all made in the new century. Playing on the theme, films like the very popular *Apocalypto* made in 2006 by Mel Gibson broadened the audience for that imagery, as did television documentaries like *Doomsday Preppers* about people preparing for the end of the world. By some count, the end-of-time book series known as *Left Behind*, about those "raptured" to the afterlife and those left behind, was the largest-selling book series of all time.

Film historians are likely to suggest that apocalypticism was introduced to American culture by the 1978 film *Apocalypse Now*. Set in Vietnam, with a storyline about conspiratorial government and military infighting, it ended in a fireball with everything blown to bits. The film by Francis Ford Coppola was popular and won two Academy Awards. But what had put the notion on the filmmaker's mind and made him think that theatergoers could be drawn to it?

The short form of the revivified apocalyptic imagery in modern America is that it was born-again and cradled in the culture of military defeat, loss of national pride, and anxiety about the future that followed the War in Vietnam. Today's apocalypticism is an end-of-empire phenomenon emanating from homes, workplaces, farms, and places of worship, cultivated by Hollywood since the 1970s, and nurtured by the neo-conservative witch-hunt for radicals and liberals responsible for the loss of the war-at-home during the 1980s and 1990s that has grown, now, to become the dominant American political narrative.

Culture critics attuned to these currents would argue that policy elites such as Steve Bannon are tapping a deep vein of uncertainty running through the country. Their light on modernism's rot is touching a nihilist impulse—think Nazi Germany. The emotional appeal of the fascist end-of-time fanaticism is a match waiting to be struck; the social conditions wrought by job loss, broken institutions, and the declining global stature of America once imagined by its masses to be their "City on the Hill" is kindling, ready to burn.

The immediate premise of Donald Trump's MAGA movement is that America was once great, and we need to return to those glory days. The war in Vietnam is the historical marker for the fall, less as a blow to America's international standing per se than as an indicator of the *internal* cultural decay responsible for the defeat, as the Trumpian nationalists understand the situation to be. The loss in Vietnam deepened American unease about its strength and moral fiber; it left the country angry, confused, and divided over why we had lost, and anxious about the future, a collapse of self-confidence seen by the whole world, averred the rightists, as evidence of national rot.

Fought to a stalemate in the 1968 Tet Offensive by an outgunned and underfed peasant army, the assumed superiority of modern military technology and intelligence came into question. The urban rebellions that swept the nation after the assassination of Civil Rights leader Martin Luther King in April of that year left the populous doubting that its racial divide could ever be bridged. The assassination of presidential candidate Robert Kennedy in June and the implosion of the Chicago Democratic National convention in August dealt blows to the centerpiece of modern democracy, the promise of peaceful transitions of power.

In the 1970s, a new generation of social theorists began writing that 1968 was the year when the limits of modernism were revealed; by the end of the 1970s modernism's promise to deliver more and better appeared chimerical, said those observers.[13] But the theorist's prognosis lacked a prescription. If modernism had run its course, what came next? Was there a path to a *post*modernism?

The MAGA movement trolls the boundaries of modernism and traditional beliefs, looking for a way out of the national malaise. Its skepticism of science is palpable; its lean toward tribalism unmistakable; its attraction to conspiracist explanations for national setbacks is evident. While the liberal left grasps at vestiges of modern institutions to stave off societal collapse, Trumpian rightists lead masses of disgruntled Americans out the backdoor of the present to a dark and dangerous future.

The crisis of America today is societal, its understanding requiring the full range of academic social science and humanities, together with efforts of journalists and culture makers, in an approach that is holistic enough to transcend even the totality of what the experts in those fields can bring.

Notes

1 Sehgal, "The Case against the Trauma Plot."
2 Robins, "Can Historians Be Traumatized by History?"
3 Roston, *Writer's Crusade*.
4 Vonnegut, *Slaughter-House Five*, 42–44.
5 Roston, *Writer's Crusade*, 145.
6 Ibid., 165, 167.
7 Ibid., 30–31, 164–166.
8 Donald Trump "Stalked" Hillary Clinton as an Intimidation Tactic (dailydot.com).
9 www.usatoday.com/story/news/politics/2020/10/28/president-donald-trump-anth ony-fauci-timeline-relationship-coronavirus-pandemic/3718797001/
10 Trump trashes Fauci and makes baseless coronavirus claims in campaign call— CNNPolitics. It was not clear what Trump meant by Fauci having been around 500 years.
11 Trump's tolerance for Traditionalism's anti-capitalism and anti-commercialism contradicts his affinity for opulent possessions. But Neil Postman pointed out in *Amusing Ourselves to Death*, 109, that in a culture of spectacles a that-was-then, this-is-now disconnect in information flow nullifies the meaning of contradiction. For his followers, his ownership of casinos in a time and place removed from the Oval Office in 2020 makes it a fact unrelated to his embrace of Traditionalism—there is no contradiction.
12 In five years after the 2003 invasion of Iraq, the *New York Times* used the word "apocalypse" in news stories alone more than 1100 times.
13 Best and Kellner, *Postmodern Theory*; Harvey, *The Condition of Post-Modernity*.

BIBLIOGRAPHY

Allen, Michael. *Until the Last Man Comes Home: POWs, MIAs, and the Unending Vietnam War*. Chapel Hill: UNC Press, 2009.

Appy, Christian G. *American Reckoning: The Vietnam War and Our National Identity*. New York: Viking, 2015.

Armstrong, Thomas and Bunmi Olatunji. "PTSD in the Media: A Critical Analysis of the Portrayal of Controversial Issues." *The Scientific Review of Mental Health Practice* 7(1): 55–60, 2009.

Bakogianni, Anastasia and Valerie M. Hope. *War as Spectacle: Ancient and Modern Perspectives on the Display of Armed Conflict*. London: Bloomsbury, 2015.

Bates, Milton. *The Wars We Took to Vietnam. Cultural Conflict and Storytelling*. Berkeley: University of California Press, 1996.

Belson, Ken. "The N.F.L.'s Other Scourge: Obesity." *The New York Times*, January 20, 2019a.

Belson, Ken. "Cheers Fade, The Pain Grows." *The New York Times*, February 3, 2019b.

Belson, Ken. "Top Concussion Panel Dismisses Links to C.T.E. Cited by Other Experts." *New York Times*, November 9, 2022.

Bensaude-Vincent, Bernadette. *Science and Spectacle in the European Enlightenment*. London: Routledge, 2008.

Best, Steven and Douglas Kellner. *Postmodern Theory: Critical Interrogations*. New York: The Guilford Press, 1991.

Biedler, Philip. "The Last Huey." *The Vietnam War and Postmodernity*. ed. Philip Biedler. Amherst, MA: UMass Press, 2–16, 1999.

Bourne, Peter. *Men, Stress, and Vietnam*. Boston: Little, Brown, 1970.

Browne, Janet. "Darwin and the Face of Madness" pp. 151–165, 1985.

Budreau, Lisa. *Bodies of War: World War I and the Politics of Commemoration in America, 1919–1933*. New York: New York University Press, 2010.

Burns, Sarah. *The Central Park Five*. New York: Vintage/Random House, 2011.

Cain, Susan. *Quiet: The Power of Introverts in a World that Can't Stop Talking*. New York: Broadway Books, 2010.

Carson, Rachel. *Silent Spring*. New York: Houghton Mifflin Company, 1962.

Caruth, Cathy. *Unclaimed Experience: Trauma, Narrative, and History.* Baltimore: Johns Hopkins University Press, 1996.

Catton, Philip E. *Diem's Final Failure: Prelude to America's War in Vietnam.* Lawrence, Kansas: University Press of Kansas, 2002.

Chancer, Lynn and Andrews, J. *The Unhappy Divorce of Sociology and Psychoanalysis: Diverse Perspectives on the Psychosocial.* New York: Palgrave, 2014.

Chute, Hillary L. *Disaster Drawn: Visual Witness, Comics, and Documentary Form.* Cambridge MA: Belknap Press/Harvard, 2016.

Clark, Constance. *God or Gorilla: Images of Evolution in the Jazz Age.* Baltimore: Johns Hopkins University Press, 2008.

Clements, Charles. *Witness to War: An American Doctor in El Salvador.* New York: Bantam Books, 1984.

Conrad, Peter and J. W. Schneider. *Deviance and Medicalization: From Badness to Sickness.* Philadelphia: Temple University Press, 1992.

Cook, Fred J. "The Real Conspiracy Exposed: Justice in Gainesville." *Nation Magazine,* 295–302, 1973.

Coyne, John R. *The Impudent Snobs: Agnew vs. the Intellectual Establishment.* New Rochelle, NY: Arlington House, 1972.

Dao, James. "Study Seeks Biomarkers for Invisible War Scars." *New York Times* February 7, p. A17, 2013.

De Jong, Alex. *Weimar Chronicles.* London: Paddington Press, 1978.

Dipple, John V.H. *War and Sex: A Brief History of Men's Urge for Battle.* Amherst, MA: Prometheus Books, 2010.

Dolgon, Cory. *Kill It To Save It: An Autopsy of Capitalism's Triumph Over Democracy.* Bristol, UK: Policy Press, 2017.

Dowd, Maureen. "Wishes as Lies." *The New York Times,* May 22, 2009.

Drukteinis, Albert. "A Head Injury Is Not a Brain Injury." *New England Psychodiagnostics On-Line Library,* 2012.

Dunn, J.C. *The War the Infantry Knew: 1914–1919.* London: James Publishing, 1987.

Eastman, Susan Lyn. *The American War in Vietnam: Cultural Memories at the Turn of the Century.* Knoxville, TN: University of Tennessee Press, 2017.

Eaton, Paul. "Casualties of the Budget Wars." *New York Times,* March 6, 2007.

Ehrhart, W.D. "I Could Not Help My Friend." *Virginia Quarterly* 70(4): 773–784, 1994.

Erichsen, John Eric. *Railway and Other Injuries of the Nervous System.* Philadelphia: Henry C. Lea, 1867.

Falusca-Zamponi, Simonetta. *Fascist Spectacle: The Aesthetics of Power in Mussolini's Italy.* Berkeley, CA: University of California Press, 2000.

Fargo, Jason. "Lessons from a Bloody Masterpiece." *The New York Times,* June 4, p. C2. 2020.

Fenn, Lenore. "Paul Atwood's Talk on November 18, 1994. Copy in possession of the author.

Frosch, Dan. "Fighting for the Right to Tell Lies." *New York Times,* May 21, 2011.

Fitzgerald, David, et al. (eds). *Not Even Past: How the United States Ends Wars.* New York: Berghahn Books, 2020.

Fonda, Jane. *My Life So Far.* New York: Random House, 2010.

Ford, Matthew and Hoskins, Andrew. *Radical War: Data, Attention, and Control in the Twenty-First Century.* New York: Oxford University Press, 2022.

Foucault, Michel. *Madness and Civilization.* New York: Random House, 1965.

Foucault, Michel. *Discipline and Punish: The Birth of the Prison*. London: Allen Lane, 1977.

Frankel, Fred. "The Concept of Flashbacks in Historical Perspective." *International Journal of Clinical and Experimental Hypnosis* 42(4):321–336, 1994.

Franklin, H. Bruce. *M.I.A. or Mythmaking in America: How and Why the Belief in Live POWs Possessed a Nation*. New York: Lawrence, 1991.

Gieryn, Thomas F. *Cultural Boundaries of Science: Credibility on the Line*. Chicago: University of Chicago Press, 1999.

Gilman, Sander L. *Seeing the Insane*. Lincoln: University of Nebraska Press, 1982.

Giroux, Henry. *Disposable Futures*. San Francisco: City Lights Open Media, 2015.

Glasser, Ronald. "A Shock Wave of Brain Injuries." *Washington Post*, April 8, 2007.

Goldin, Rebecca and Cindy Merrick. "Neuroscience or Neurobabble?: What's This Thing Called fMRI? 2012. STATS. Fairfax, VA, July 16.

Graeber, David and David Wengrow. *The Dawn of Everything: A New History of Humanity*. New York: Farrar, Straus and Giroux, 2021.

Grinker, Lori. "UK's Royal Society Report [on PTSD]." Ochberg Society for Trauma Journalism. November, 2012.

Hagopian, Patrick. *The Vietnam War in American Memory: Veterans, Memorials, and the Politics of Healing*. Amherst, MA: University of Massachusetts Press, 2009.

Hamilton, Richard. *Who Voted for Hitler?* Princeton: Princeton University Press, 1982.

Harrington, Anne. *The Cure Within: A History of Mind–Body Medicine*. New York: W.W. Norton, 2008.

Harris, Robert and Jeremy Paxman. *A Higher Form of Killing*. New York: Random House, 1983.

Harvey, David. *The Condition of Post-Modernity*. London: Wiley-Blackwell, 1991.

Hautzinger, Sarah and Jean Scandlyn. *Beyond Post-Traumatic Stress: Homefront Struggles with the War on Terror*. Walnut Creek, CA: Left Coast Press, 2014.

Hochschild, Adam. *To End All Wars*. New York: Houghton Mifflin Harcourt/Mariner Books, 2011.

Hoge, Charles W. *Navigating the Transition from Combat to Home: Including Combat Stress, PTSD, and mTBI*. Guilford, CT: Globe Pequet Press, 2010.

Horkheimer, Max and Theodor Adorno. *Dialectic of Enlightenment*. New York: Continuum/Seabury Press, 1944.

Howes, Craig. *Voices of the Vietnam POWs: Witnesses to Their Fight*. New York: Oxford University Press, 1993.

Hunt, Andrew. *The Turning: A History of Vietnam Veterans against the War*. New York: NYU Press, 1999.

Hyer, Lee et al. "Suicidal Behavior among Chronic Vietnam Theatre Veterans with PTSD." *Journal of Clinical Psychology* 46(6): 713–721, 1990.

Jonathan, Simon. "Honore Fragonard, Anatomical Virtuoso" in Bensaude-Vincent and Blondel, *War as pectacle:Ancient and Modern Perspectives on the Displays of Armed Conflict*, pp. 141–158. London: Bloomsbury, 2015.

Kaes, Anton. *Shell Shock Cinema: Weimar Culture and the Wounds of War*. Princeton: Princeton University Press, 2011.

Kaplan, Robert D. *Adriatic: A Concept of Civilization at the End of the Modern Era*. New York: Random House, 2022.

Kifner, John. "Veterans Face Guardsmen in Protest at Miami Beach." *New York Times*, August 22, p. 36, 1972.

Klare, Michael. "Saying Goodbye to Planet Earth?" tomdispatch.com, May 23, 2022.

Kracauer, Siegfried. *From Caligari to Hitler: A Psychological History of German Film*. Princeton: Princeton University Press, 1947.

Kristoff, Nicholas. "War Wounds." *New York Times*, August 10, 2012.

Kulik, Gary. *War Stories: False Atrocity Stories, Swift Boaters, and Winter Soldiers—What Really Happened in Vietnam*. Washington, D.C.: Potomac Books, 2009.

Lair, Meredith. *Armed with Abundance: Consumerism & Soldiering in the Vietnam War*. Chapel Hill: University of North Carolina Press, 2011.

LeBon, Gustave. *The Crowd a Study of the Popular Mind*. Kessinger Books, 1876.

Leed, Eric. *No Man's Land: Combat and Identity in World War I*. New York: Cambridge University, 1979.

Lembcke, Jerry. *The Spitting Image: Myth, Memory, and the Legacy of Vietnam*. New York: NYU Press, 1998.

Lembcke, Jerry. "The Facts about Soldiers' Ages." *National Catholic Reporter*, May 25, 2007a.

Lembcke, Jerry. "The Horror of War Can Be Catnip for Young Men." *National Catholic Reporter*, March 25, 2007b.

Lembcke, Jerry. *Hanoi Jane: War, Sex, and Fantasies of Betrayal*. Amherst, MA: University of Massachusetts Press, 2010.

Lembcke, Jerry. *PTSD: Diagnosis and Identity in Post-empire America*. Lanham, MD: Lexington Books, 2013a.

Lembcke, Jerry. "Flashbacks, Fireworks…. and Cars that Backfire?" *CounterPunch*, July 11, 2013b.

Lembcke, Jerry. "War Trauma and the *The New York Times*" April 17, 2014.

Leys, Ruth. *Trauma: A Genealogy*. Chicago: University of Chicago Press, 2000.

Longerich, Peter. *Heinrich Himmler*. New York: Oxford University Press, 2012.

Lynd, Alice and Staughton Lynd. *Moral Injury and Nonviolent Resistance: Breaking the Cycle of Violence in the Military and Behind Bars*. Oakland, CA: PM Press, 2017.

Lynn, Edward J. and Mark Belza. "Factitious Posttraumatic Stress Disorder: The Veteran Who Never Got to Vietnam." *Hospital and Community Psychiatry* 35: 697–701, 1984.

MacMillan, Margaret. "Neither War Nor Peace: A New Look at the Aftermath of World War I." *The New York Times*. December 11, 2016.

Malo, Jean-Jacques and Tony Williams. *Vietnam War Films*. Jefferson, NC: McFarland, 1994.

Martini, Edwin. *Agent Orange: History, Science, and the Politics of Uncertainty*. Amherst, MA: UMass Press, 2012.

May, Elaine Tyler. *Fortress America: How We Embraced Fear and Abandoned Democracy*. New York: Basic Books, 2017.

Meili, Trisha. *I Am the Central Park Jogger: A Story of Hope and Possibility*. New York: Scribner, 2003.

McConnell, Justine. "Epic Parodies: Martial Extravaganzas on the Nineteenth-Century Stage" in *Bakogianni and Hope*, , Eds, London: Bloomsbury, 257–270, 2015.

Milam, Ron. *The Vietnam War in Popular Culture: The Influence of America's Most Controversial War on Everyday Life*. Denver: Praeger, 2017.

Moser, Richard. *The New Winter Soldiers: GI and Veteran Dissent during the Vietnam Era*. New Brunswick, NJ: Rutgers University Press, 1996.

Murphy, Kate. "Do You Believe in God, or Is That a Software Glitch?" *New York Times*, August 28, p. SR5, 2016.

Myers, Tobias. "What if We Had a War and *Everybody* Came?": War as Spectacle and Duel of Iliad 3" in *Bakogianni and Hope*, Eds, London: Bloomsbury, 15–42, 2015.

News Release. "Vietnam Peace Parade Committee Schedules Massive Protest Aug. 6." Fifth Avenue Peace Parade Committee. Wisconsin State Historical Society Library, Madison, 1966.

Nordheimer, Jon. "From Dak To to Detroit: Death of a Troubled Vietnam Hero." *New York Times*, November 9, p. A1, 1971.

Nordheimer, Jon. "Postwar Shock Besets Ex-GIs." *New York Times*, August 21, p. A1, 1972.

O'Sullivan, Suzanne. *The Sleeping Beauties: And Other Stories if Mystery Illness.* New York: Pantheon Books, 2021.

Postman, Neil. *Amusing Ourselves to Death: Public Discourse in the Age of Show Business.* New York: Penguin, 1985.

Reid, Fiona. *Broken Men: Shell Shock Treatment and Recovery in Britain 1914–1930.* New York: Continuum Books, 2010.

Rieckhoff, Paul. *Big Think* . Bigthink.com 2010.

Robins, James. "Can Historians Be Traumatized by History?" *The New Republic*, February 2, 2021.

Roston, Tom. *Writer's Crusade: Kurt Vonnegut and the Many Lives of Slaughterhouse-Five.* New York: Abrams Press, 2021.

Roth, Michael S. *Memory, Trauma, and History: Essays on Living with the Past.* New York: Columbia University Press, 2012.

Schyeldahl, Peter. "Hitler as Artist: How Vienna Inspired the Fuhrer's Dreams." *The New Yorker*, August 19, 2002.

Scott, Linda M. "Spectacular Vernacular: Literacy and Commercial Culture in the Postmodern Age." *International Journal of Research in Marketing* 10: 251–275, 1993.

Scott, Wilbur. *The Politics of Readjustment: Vietnam Veterans Since the War.* New York: Aldine de Gruyter, 1993.

Sehgal, Parul. "The Case against the Trauma Plot," *The New Yorker Magazine*, December 27, 2021.

Shatan, Chaim. "Post-Vietnam Syndrome." *New York Times*, May 6, L35, 1972.

Shaw, Irwin. *Bury The Dead.* 1936.

Shay, Jonathan, M.D. *Achilles in Vietnam: Combat Trauma and the Undoing of Character.* New York: Simon and Schuster, 1994.

Shay, Jonathon, M.D. "Betrayal of 'What's Right': Vietnam Combat Veterans and Post-traumatic Stress Disorder." *The Long Term View: Legacies of Vietnam* 5(1): 81–91, 2002.

Shephard, Ben. *A War of Nerves: Soldiers and Psychiatrists in the Twentieth Century.* Cambridge, MA: Harvard University Press, 2001.

Shirer, William. *Rise and Fall of the Third Reich: A History of Nazi Germany.* New York: Simon and Schuster, 1960.

Showalter, Elaine. *Hysteries: Hysterical Epidemics and Modern Media.* New York: Columbia University Press, 1997.

Southhard, Elmer Ernest. *Shell-Shock and Other Neuropsychiatric Problems.* Goodpress publishing.com, 2019.

Spar, Landy and Loren D. Pankratz. "Factitious Posttraumatic Stress Disorder." *American Journal of Psychiatry* 140: 1016–1019, 1983.

Speer, Albert. *Inside the Third Reich: Memoirs.* New York: Macmillan, 1970.

Starr, Paul. *The Discarded Army: Veterans after Vietnam.* New York: Charterhouse, 1973a.

Starr, Paul. "Home from the War—Vietnam Veterans: Neither Victims nor Executioners." *Worldview*, 53–55, Home (worldviewmagazine.com), October, 1973b.

Steinhauer, Jennifer. "For Veterans, the Trauma Doesn't End with Service." *The New York Times*, September 12, 2021.

Stone, Martin. "Shellshock and the Psychologists" in W.F. Bynum, Roy Porter, and Michael Shepherd *The Anatomy of Medicine*. Cambridge: Tavistock Publications, 242–271, 1885.

Taylor, Philip. *Fragments of the Present: Searching for Modernity in Vietnam's South*. Honolulu, University of Hawai'I Press, 2001.

Teitelbaum, Benjamin. *War for Eternity: Inside Bannon's Far-Right Circle of Power Brokers*. New York: Dey Street Books, 2020.

Theweleit, Klaus. *Women, Floods, Bodies, History*. Vol. 1 of *Male Fantasies*. Minneapolis: University of Minnesota Press, 1987.

Thiele, Leslie Paul. *Environmentalism for a New Millennium: The Challenge of Coevolution*. New York: Oxford University Press, 1999.

Trumbo, Dalton. *Johnny Got His Gun*. New York: Bantam Books, 1967.

Turse, Nick. *Kill Anything that Moves: The Real American War in Vietnam*. New York: Henry Holt, 2013.

Vonnegut, Kurt Jr. *Slaughter-House Five*. New York: Dell, 1971.

War Office Great Britain. *Report of the War Office Committee of Enquiry into "Shell-Shock*. London: His Majesty's Stationary Office, 1922.

Wells, Tom. *The War Within: America's Battle over Vietnam*. Berkeley: University of California Press, 1994.

Wilber, Tom and Jerry Lembcke. *Dissenting POWs: From Vietnam's Hoa Lo Prison to America Today*. New York: Monthly Review Press, 2021.

Wilcox, Fred A. *Scorched Earth Legacies of Chemical Warfare in Vietnam*. New York: Seven Stories Press, 2011.

Wingo, Hal. "From GIs in Vietnam, Unexpected Cheers." *Life*, October 24, p. 36, 1969.

Winter, Jay. *Sites of Memory and Mourning: The Great War in European Cultural History*. Cambridge: Cambridge University Press, 1995.

Woodruff, Bob. *In an Instant: A Family's Journey through Love and Healing*. New York: Random House, 2006.

Young, Allan. *The Harmony of Illusions: Inventing Post-traumatic Stress Disorder*. Princeton, NJ: Princeton University Press, 1997.

Zeitlin, Irving. *Ideology and the Development of Sociological Theory* (7th edition). New York: Prentice Hall, 2001.

Zierler, David. *The Invention of Ecocide: Agent Orange, Vietnam, and the Scientists Who Changed the Way We Think about the Environment*. Athens: University of Georgia Press, 2010.

Zulaika, Joseba. *Hellfire from Paradise Ranch: On the Frontlines of Drone Warfare*. Berkeley: University of California Press.

FILMOGRAPHY

The Activist. 1969. Regional Films. 85 mins.

All Quiet on the Western Front. 1930. U.S.A. Universal. 2hrs. 27 mins.

Alice's Restaurant. 1969. MGM. 111 mins.

Apocalypse. 2012. Canada. 46 mins.

Apocalypse Now. 1979. U.S.A. United Artists-Zoetrope. 153 mins.

Apocalypse World War II. 2009. France. CC&C. 5hrs. 12 mins.

Apocalypto. 2006. U.S.A. Icon Productions. 2hrs. 19 mins.

The Best Year of Our Lives. 1946. U.S.A. Samuel Goldwyn Company. 2hrs. 52 mins.

Black Sunday. 1977. U.S.A. Paramount. 143 mins.

Blackhawk Down. 2001. U.S.A. Revolution Studios. 2hrs. 32 mins.

Blood of Ghastly Horror, 1975–1972. U.S.A. Independence International Pictures Corporation. Color, 86 mins.

Born on the Fourth of July. 1989. U.S.A. Ixtian. 2hrs. 25 mins.

Brother from Another Planet. 1984. U.S.A. Anarchist Convention Films. 1hr. 48 mins.

Bus Riley's Back in Town. 1971. U.S.A. William Thompson International. 93 mins.

The Cabinet of Dr. Caligari. 1920. Germany. Decla-Bioscop AG. 1hr. 7 mins.

Coming Home. 1978. U.S.A. United Artists. 128 mins.

Da Five Bloods. 2020. U.S.A. 40 Acres & A Mule Filmworks. 2hrs. 34 mins.

Death Dream. 1972. Canada. Alpha. 89 mins.

Don't Look Up. 2021. U.S.A. Hyperprojects Industries. 2hrs. 18 mins.

First Blood. 1982. U.S.A. Orion. 96 mins.

Four Horsemen of The Apocalypse. 1921. Canada. Metro Pictures. Silent. 2hrs. 30 mins.

From Here to Eternity. 1953. U.S.A. Columbia. 1hr. 58 mins.

FTA. 1972. U.S.A. Free Theater Associates/Indochina Peace Campaign.

Full Metal Jacket. 1987. U.S.A. Warner Brothers. 118 mins.

Getting Straight. 1970. Columbia. 125 mins.

The Green Berets. 1968. U.S.A. Werner Brothers–Seven Arts. 141 mins.

Greetings. 1968. U.S.A. West End Films. 88 mins.

Hamburger Hill. 1987. U.S.A. RKO Pictures. 110 mins.

The Hurt Locker. 2008. U.S.A. 2hrs. 7 mins.

High Sierra. 1941. U.S.A. Warner Bros. 1hr. 40 mins.

Jarhead. 2005. U.S.A. Universal. 2hrs. 5 mins.

Johnny Got His Gun. 1971. U.S.A. Cinemation. 1hr. 51 mins.

Let There Be Light. 1946. U.S.A. U.S. Army. 58 mins.

Lions for Lambs. 2007. U.S.A. MGM. 1hr. 32 mins.

The Lively Set. 1964. U.S.A. Universal. 95 mins.

Maltese Falcon. 1941. U.S.A. Warner Bros. 1hr. 20 mins.

Manchurian Candidate. 1962. U.S.A. M.C. Productions. 2hrs. 6 mins.

Motor Psycho. 1965. U.S.A. Eve Productions. 73 mins.

Platoon. 1986. U.S.A. Hemdale. 120 mins.

The Pursuit of D.B. Cooper. 1981. U.S.A. Universal/MCA. Color. 100 mins.

The Rack. 1956. U.S.A. MGM. 1hr. 40 mins.

Red Badge of Courage. 1951. U.S.A. MGM. 1hr. 9 mins.

The Return of The Secaucus Seven. U.S.A. Salsepuedes Productions. 1hr. 44 mins.

The Revolutionary. 1970. U.S.A. United Artists. 101 mins.

Ruckus. 1980. U.S.A. International Vision, Inc. Color, 91 mins.

Sands of Iwo Jima. 1949. U.S.A. Republic Pictures. 1hr. 40 mins.

Science Odyssey: In Search of Ourselves. U.S.A. Public Broadcasting System.

Sir! No Sir! 2005. U.S.A. Displaced Films. 1hr. 25 mins.

Stop Loss. 2008. Paramount. 1hr. 52 mins.

The Stunt Man. 1980. U.S.A. Twentieth-Century Fox. Color, 90 mins.

Taxi Driver. 1976. U.S.A. Columbia. 130 mins.

Three Kings. 1999. U.S.A. 1hr. 54 mins.

Time Limit. 1957. U.S.A. Heath Productions. 1hr. 36 mins.

Unnatural Causes. 1986. U.S.A. ITC. 2hrs.

In the Valley of Elah. 2007. U.S.A. Warner. 2hrs. 1 min.

The Vietnam War. 2017. U.S.A. PBS. 18 Episodes.

Zombie Apocalypse. 2012. UK. Firecracker Films. 1hr. 27 mins.

The Visitors. 1972. U.S.A. United Artists. 1hr. 28 mins.

Witness to War. 1985 U.S.A. 29 mins.

INDEX

Printed in the United States
by Baker & Taylor Publisher Services